THE CHILD WITCHES OF OLAGUE

MAGIC *in* HISTORY

SOURCEBOOKS SERIES

The Magic in History Sourcebooks series features compilations and translations of key primary texts that illuminate specific aspects of the history of magic and the occult from within. Each title is tightly focused, but the scope of the series is chronologically and geographically broad, ranging from ancient to modern and with a global reach. Selections are in readable and reliable English, annotated where necessary, with brief contextualizing introductions.

SERIES EDITORS

RICHARD KIECKHEFER,
Northwestern University

CLAIRE FANGER,
Rice University

THE CHILD WITCHES OF OLAGUE

LU ANN HOMZA

The Pennsylvania State University Press

University Park, Pennsylvania

Library of Congress Cataloging-in-Publication Data

Names: Homza, Lu Ann, 1958– author.
Title: The child witches of Olague / Lu Ann Homza.
Other titles: Magic in history sourcebooks series.
Description: University Park, Pennsylvania : The Pennsylvania State University Press, [2024] | Series: Magic in history sourcebooks series | Includes bibliographical references and index.
Summary: "Examines village interactions in the witch-hunt that tormented Navarre from 1608–1614. Includes the legal depositions of self-described child-witches, their parents, and their victims, illuminating the social, familial, and legal tragedies that could accompany witchcraft suspicions and accusations"—Provided by publisher.
Identifiers: LCCN 2024005983 | ISBN 9780271098807 (hardback) | ISBN 9780271097497 (paperback)
Subjects: LCSH: Witchcraft—Spain—Olagüe—History—17th century—Sources. | Trials (Witchcraft)—Spain—Olagüe—History—17th century—Sources. | LCGFT: Primary sources.
Classification: LCC BF1584.S7 H657 2024 | DDC 133.4/3094652—dc23/eng/20240318
LC record available at https://lccn.loc.gov/2024005983

THIS BOOK IS DEDICATED TO MY STUDENTS,
PAST, PRESENT, FUTURE.

CONTENTS

MAP 1 Important witch-hunting sites in northeast Spain, 1608–14. Map created by Mike Bechthold.

ACKNOWLEDGMENTS

I am delighted to thank the people and institutions who helped create this book. My first appreciation goes to archivists in Pamplona: without their discoveries and assistance, the sources translated here would never have come to light. In 2014 and 2018, experts at the Archivo Real y General de Navarra (AGN) found two previously uncatalogued legal cases from the early seventeenth century. Dated 1611–12, the two cases were conducted by the royal secular court in Pamplona, but their complaints originated in the tiny village of Olague, twelve miles away: they were lawsuits for slander in which one adult called another a witch. The two trials turned out to be fallout from one of the most notorious witch hunts in European history, which afflicted the region of Navarre from December 1608 through 1614. That witch persecution resulted in literally thousands of suspects, with eleven convicted witches burned at the stake in 1610. By 1614, the Spanish Inquisition, which was in charge of the persecution, decided not only to revise its instructions for prosecuting witches but also to annul its own verdicts and cases against the Navarrese witch suspects whom it had sentenced over the previous six years.

The recently discovered trials from Olague have several extraordinary characteristics and greatly add to our understanding of local dynamics in this witch persecution. They contain multiple depositions by self-identified child witches, who publicly and repeatedly accused adults of witchcraft and thereby dishonored them; at least two adults died as a result of the children's actions. These cases make it clearer than ever that children were the driving force in this witch hunt. Furthermore, the cases from Olague feature adult defendants who launched their own countersuits for defamation. As a result, the evidentiary record becomes much more complex and revealing with regard to coerced confessions and accusations of witchcraft, village factions, and familial discord. The Olague trials only surfaced because the archivists at the AGN are so diligent. My heartfelt thanks to Miriam Etxeberria, Berta Elcano, Félix Segura Urra, and Peio Monteano Sorbet. As has been the case with my other publications, Peio generously went through the manuscript to verify that people and place names accorded with modern Basque spellings that modern readers would recognize.

Meanwhile, in the Archivo Diocesano de Pamplona (ADP), archivist Teresa Alzugaray helped me to discover in 2019 a basically unknown petition for a marital separation in Olague that also had the larger witch hunt in Navarre as its essential context. This petition to separate was successful. It was launched by a wife who had been accused of witchcraft in 1611 by her adolescent, child witch daughter, who only named her mother because she had been threatened by her father and a stepbrother into making the allegations. The petition and its witnesses offer remarkable insights about gender norms and domestic violence in early modern Navarre and illustrate how gender and matrimonial discord could intersect with witch hunting. I am so thankful to Teresa for knowing where to look in the records of the ADP and to the ADP's former archivist Don José Luis Sales Tirapu for having created index-card files on the entire archive, broken down by location.

In Virginia, the former dean of Arts & Sciences at William & Mary Kate Conley supported my research on this witch hunt in every conceivable way between 2013 and 2017. I am grateful to Keith and Sandy Dauer for generously supporting the travel and research efforts of our History Department faculty. Thanks to the Roy R. Charles Center for Academic Excellence at William & Mary, I received a Margaret S. Glauber Fellowship in 2020–21, which allowed two undergraduates to work with me on conceptualizing this primary source reader. Cayla J. Harrison and Madeline Covington were fantastic research assistants and spoke eloquently about our work to several different audiences. We thank Mrs. Glauber most sincerely for making our collaboration possible. Later, two more stellar undergraduates, Emma Herber and

Isabel Pereira-López, read over a draft of the book and offered helpful comments.

Thank you to the series editors of Magic in History Sourcebooks, Richard Kieckhefer and Claire Fanger, for accepting this project, as well as to Eleanor Goodman, executive editor at Pennsylvania State University Press, for her guidance and assistance. My thanks to Mike Bechthold for creating another excellent map.

I am lucky to have a crew that is interested in archival research and always willing to talk about it. So many thanks to Thomas B. Payne, Amanda L. Scott, and Celeste I. McNamara, as well as Christopher Homza, Wendy Williams, and Lisa Esposito: you are cherished.

Introduction

From 1608 to 1614, thousands of children across Navarre labeled themselves as child witches through the term *haur-sorgina* in Basque, which the legal systems rendered into Spanish as *niño embrujado* for male child witches or *niña embrujada* for female ones. This new identity held true whether the children in question were speaking in their homes, in public, or in court. The youngsters blamed their condition on older witches who lived nearby, snatched them from their beds, and took them to meet the Devil. The child witches' claims provoked one of the largest witch hunts in European history, one that resulted in the suffering of thousands of people, the rewriting of formal instructions for Spanish inquisitors, and the nullification of legal verdicts by the Spanish Inquisition.[1]

The type of witchcraft in play over this six-year period conformed in many ways to long-standing traditions about witches in Navarre. Custom stipulated that Navarrese witches could be either men or women, who could fly through the air to the Devil's gatherings.[2] Navarre's witches took oaths of loyalty to the Devil; they turned toads into poisons, destroyed harvests, and murdered children.[3] Yet the paradigm that dominated the 1608–14 witch hunt pushed conventions to unprecedented lengths. In 1608–14, the witches openly worshiped the Devil in gatherings rendered as *akelarreak* in Basque and *akelar-res* in Spanish. They participated in an upside-down Catholic Mass,

1. The classic study of this witch hunt is Henningsen, *Witches' Advocate*. For a revisionist account based on new archival sources, Homza, *Village Infernos*.

2. Historians believe the concept of a Devil's sabbat, where many of his followers gathered, helped allow for the possibility of male witches. Rowlands, "Witchcraft and Gender," 454–55.

3. Most scholars no longer believe that the witchcraft paradigm was imposed by elites from above on the masses below. As one famous historian has noted, anyone in early modern Europe could tell a story about the Devil and his followers. Briggs, *Witches and Neighbors*, 28.

wherein the Devil decried the evil they had failed to do, sang a liturgy with nonsensical words and a tuneless voice, and gave them a black wafer rather than a white one to consume. The *akelarres* featured sex between the Devil and his disciples; they also involved cannibalism when the witches consumed bodies that they had disinterred. Finally, the witches skinned toads in the *akelarres* to produce toxic substances, which they used to destroy the agriculture that sustained their communities. The full-fledged version of the witches' sabbat in Navarre between 1608 and 1614 was the most extreme in western Europe in its level of detail and depth of inversion of Christian and community values. It was unique in its alleged cannibalism of adults.[4]

From 1608 to 1614, children brought to *akelarres* immediately viewed themselves as child witches, even if they did not renounce their Christianity. In fact, the Devil often waited to demand that renunciation, because he wanted to be sure the youngsters were mature enough to know what they were doing. If he gauged them as too young, he still found them useful: his witches put them in charge of guarding herds of ordinary toads, as well as toads that wore clothing. The groups of toads had different purposes. The witches turned the ordinary ones into poison; the clothed ones acted as diabolical guardian angels who awakened their witches to go to the *akelarres* and expelled the

---

4. The concept of the Devil's sabbat was created by 1450 in western Europe, but its features varied widely across time and space. In Germany and the Netherlands, the Devil's reunions often simply mirrored village dances and local social hierarchies: Briggs, *Witches and Neighbors*, 40–41; Blécourt, "Sabbath Stories," 86; Roper, *Witch Craze*, 110–11. In Finnmark, the Devil's gatherings lacked sex or cannibalism: Hagen, "Witchcraft Criminality," 389–90. In Germany, suspects' confessions about the Devil's gatherings were pared down unless torture was involved: Roper, *Witch Craze*, 69–81, 82–120. The judge and demonologist Pierre de Lancre's description of the witches' sabbats in the French Basque country in 1609 corresponds in some ways to Navarrese ones from 1609 to 1612, with flight, toads, a feast that disappeared, indiscriminate sex, and renunciations of the Christian God. Yet de Lancre's account also differs: abducted children put up no resistance, the Devil's appearance constantly changed, witches shape-shifted into animals, and there were many fewer details on the diabolical Mass. Moreover, de Lancre insisted that French Basque witches focused on weather magic and often flew to Newfoundland, which was befitting, given the area's maritime economy: de Lancre, *On the Inconstancy of Witches*, 96–97, 99–100, 119, 151, 155–56, 158.

ointment that allowed them to fly there. Aside from guarding toads, even the child witches who accepted the Devil as their god primarily acted as witnesses to the witches' plans and actions. Some female child witches, typically teenagers, told legal authorities that they had experienced sex with the Devil.[5] More children of all ages said they had watched the Devil's fornication with adults, as well as the witches' formulations of poisons. Still, the surviving documentation from and about child witches rarely attests their participation in harmful magic and never features them engaging in cannibalism.

It is crucial to note that in this particular witch hunt and in Navarrese witchcraft in general, child witches were treated as victims by their communities, even when they had renounced their Christianity before the Devil.[6] Crucial conditions for their innocent status were a very young age—which implied a lack of consent—as well as the insistence that they had been taken to meet the Devil against their will. Boys fourteen and over and girls twelve and over could be in legal trouble if they had been seen at a Devil's *akelarre* but neglected to say they had been forcibly transported there.[7]

The court systems in Navarre generally agreed with local communities and sidestepped the prosecution of child witches, though there were exceptions.[8] When it came to adults practicing witchcraft, however, there were three legal jurisdictions in Navarre (and Spain) that cared about their punishment and correction. When witches caused bodily injuries to people, animals, or crops through harmful magic, the royal secular court in Pamplona, under the supervision of the royal viceroy, could prosecute them. When witches renounced

5. While the Devil allegedly had sex with both his female and male followers, as all the child witches insisted, I have not found a male child witch or teenage-witch who admitted to copulating with him.

6. For contrasting attitudes on the guilt of child witches in Scandinavia, Switzerland, and Germany, see Willumsen, "Children Accused of Witchcraft," 30–33; Bettlé, "Child-Witches"; Roper, *Witch Craze*, 204–21. From 1609 through 1611, Spanish inquisitors in

Logroño treated the statements of child witches as reliable testimony. Homza, *Village Infernos*, 96–97.

7. Homza, *Village Infernos*, 22–23.

8. In 1595, the secular court in Pamplona imprisoned three girls as witches, and the Spanish Inquisition declined to intervene. Although the children eventually were released to a hospital, they died. Archivo Real y General de Navarra (AGN), *Tribunales reales*, #71319. Rojas, "Bad Christians and Hanging Toads," 97–100.

their Christian baptism to venerate the Devil, the episcopal court, headed by Pamplona's bishop, worried about their religious welfare, because the Devil was the archenemy of the Christian God.

Nevertheless, a Spanish bishop's interest in witches was typically superseded by the Spanish Inquisition's. With witches' worship of the Devil and the abandonment of their baptismal vows, they were committing heresy, and Spanish Inquisition was founded in 1478 to pursue exactly that sin. Heresy has been a concern for Christians since the founding of Christianity. By the thirteenth century, heresy was defined as a stubbornly held and publicly voiced error against Catholic theology and ritual. Only baptized Christians could be heretics; heresy had to be intentional rather than accidental, though it could also be read into hypothetical statements and dietary choices.[9] Like the ad hoc inquisitions of the medieval epoch, the Spanish Inquisition was grounded in ancient Roman law and depended on investigations carried out through human efforts.

By the early seventeenth century, Spanish inquisitors were specialists in canon law. They oversaw investigations, interrogated witnesses and defendants, held court proceedings in their tribunals, and pronounced sentences.[10] An inquisitorial inquiry could begin as a result of ordinary men and women denouncing the spiritual errors or wrongdoing of relatives, neighbors, or acquaintances. An investigation also could start through information sent to inquisitors by their employees in the field. A defendant's guilt was presumed in the inquisitorial system, as it was in the secular and episcopal courts. While defendants in inquisition trials were assigned a lawyer and had

9. For the Inquisition's procedures and targets, see Homza, *Spanish Inquisition*. Spanish inquisitors were interested in learning about witches' harmful magic because it enhanced the witches' possible connections to the Devil. Still, it was the witches' religious apostasy that was the grounds for inquisitorial prosecution. Spanish inquisitors went after a range of heretics, such as individuals who observed Jewish or Islamic rituals despite being baptized Christians, preferred Protestant Christianity, or indulged in morals offenses, such as bigamy. The last category seemed to demonstrate wrong religious belief about the sacrament of marriage.

10. Spanish inquisitors also had two bodies of external consultants. One looked over the evidence before a trial began and assessed its degree of potential heresy; the other conferred with the inquisitors over sentencing. The latter group was supposed to include a representative of the local bishop.

access to the testimony against them, depositions were stricken of all specifics that could allow defendants to identify prosecution witnesses.

At the same time, conclusive legal proof for inquisitors was supposed to come down to two eyewitnesses to the same event or a confession. Eyewitnesses to different events amounted to partial proof, and no amount of partial proof could ever add up to a complete proof. Confession was called the "queen of proofs" because it held the highest probative value in Roman law. When Spanish inquisitors deployed torture, their aim was to gain a confession.

The Spanish Inquisition's explicit mission was to reconcile baptized Christians who had strayed from Catholicism back to the papal church. That goal explains why their officials called their sentences "penances." Typical penances might involve attending a certain number of Masses or reciting certain prayers. The guilty could be forced to wear a penitential robe, called a *sambenito*, whenever they left the house. They could be enclosed in monasteries or convents or exiled for specific periods of time. They also could be executed if they refused to confess despite conclusive proof, though again, modern scholars believe that death sentences were far rarer between 1550 and 1650 than in the first decades of the Spanish Inquisition's operation. Inquisitors were forbidden to shed blood; their sentences of execution were carried out by secular authorities.

The Spanish Inquisition officially supervised the 1608–14 witch hunt in Navarre. The inquisitors involved were located in a tribunal in the Castilian city of Logroño, approximately 104 miles southwest from the first witchcraft accusations, which occurred in the village of Zugarramurdi. Logroño's inquisitors received news about Zugarramurdi's witches in early 1609, and they quickly brought alleged leaders to their tribunal for questioning. Later the same year, one of them went into Navarre to look for witch suspects and returned with three hundred confessions. Over November 7–8, 1610, in a public ceremony called an *auto de fe*, or "act of faith," Logroño's inquisitors publicly sentenced twenty-nine individuals from Navarre for the heresy of witchcraft; they also privately sentenced two Navarrese clerics for the same offense. Out of a total of thirty-one condemned witches—nineteen female, twelve male—twenty repented and were reconciled to the Catholic Church, though most had to perform significant penances. Eleven who had refused to confess and repent were burned at the stake, six in person and five in effigy because they had already died in prison. Whether they were penanced or executed, all thirty-one witches also had their property confiscated. The Inquisition's confiscation of property was routine for convicted heretics, but it also was practically unheard of in inquisition trials for witchcraft.[11]

Contemporaries claimed that thirty thousand people attended the *auto de fe*, and two printed pamphlets about the event appeared in January 1611.[12] What happened next was a perfect storm of official inaction and local fury. Witchcraft accusations and confessions continued to flood Navarre, but the inquisitors could not possibly bring in so many suspects for trial: not only were they understaffed and underfunded, but their secret prison could not hold so many defendants. While the inquisitors' supervisors in Madrid suggested repeatedly that they go once more on visitation, this time with an edict of grace—which would have allowed them to reconcile suspects to the church without trials—they declined to do so.[13] Instead, from November 1610 through May 1611, Logroño's inquisitors remained in their tribunal and only handled witches already in custody or ones who made the long and arduous trek to the tribunal.

So long as the inquisitors continued to be absent, there seemed to be no legal solution to the witch problem in Navarre's villages. Ultimately, parents verbally and then physically attacked accused witches to force them to confess and stop them from carrying children away. Witch suspects of all ages, whether male and female, were stoned, hung from bridges, tied into trees, chained, starved, knifed, and even tortured to death. Once suspects admitted to being witches, they were in a ruinous spiritual state. They could not receive the ecclesiastical sacraments until they were absolved by an inquisitor or

11. On the question of confiscating a convicted witch's property, see Monter, *Frontiers of Heresy*, chap. 12.

12. Juan de Mongastón printed one pamphlet in Logroño on January 6, 1611. Juan Baptista Varesio printed a second one, not indebted to Mongastón's, in Burgos on January 8, 1611. The Mongastón pamphlet exists in a

modern edition—Fernández Nieto, *Proceso a la brujería*, 30–72—but we have only a single copy of the Varesio pamphlet, in Pamplona's Universidad Pública de Navarra.

13. For the important differences between an edict of faith and an edict of grace, see Homza, *Village Infernos*, 108.

a representative of Pamplona's bishop.[14] At the same time, the harshness of the Inquisition's verdicts in November 1610 had terrified the Navarrese. Families consequently brought tremendous pressure to confess on members named as witches by kin or neighbors, even when they knew the confessions would be false. They believed that if their children or relatives confessed at once, they could avoid being sent to Logroño's inquisition tribunal and having their property confiscated.

The vigilante justice that occurred across Navarre from 1609 through 1611 was illegal in every respect. Later, villagers would tell the Royal Court that they had acted out of desperation and on the advice of the Inquisition's own local employees, who had recommended they coerce witch suspects into confessions. When those inquisition employees deposed in the Royal Court in 1612—from which they were legally exempt because of their inquisitorial jobs—they explained that they had finally told villagers to force witch suspects into confessions because they could not secure peace any other way.[15]

By February 1611, the inquisitors told their superiors in Madrid that they had reports of more than fifteen hundred witch suspects. Accordingly, the Inquisition leadership finally commanded one of them to visit Navarre with an edict of grace, which would allow remorseful witch suspects to return to the Catholic Church. The visitation fell to the most junior member of the Logroño tribunal, Alonso de Salazar Frías. Salazar left in May 1611 and returned in January 1612. While he was in the field, he reconciled hundreds of alleged witches and pronounced exorcisms, as a precaution, over thousands of bewitched children. He also came to believe that his tribunal lacked sufficient evidence to prosecute current suspects for witchcraft. While he was away, Salazar heard children and adults say that they had no idea how they were taken to revere the Devil. He listened to eighty-one

---

14. Homza, *Village Infernos*, 48–49. Members of the Society of Jesus, whom the bishop of Pamplona sent into Navarre after the November 1610 *auto de fe*, did not dare to absolve and reconcile witch suspects for fear of encroachment on the Inquisition's privileges: Homza, *Village Infernos*, 102.

15. A prosecutor for the secular court attempted to have one of those inquisition employees charged with murder when a witch died in his custody: Homza, "When Witches Litigate," 261–65. For those inquisition employees' depositions in secular court, see AGN, *Tribunales reales* #072902, fols. 50r, 191r.

individuals revoke admissions to witchcraft because they had been forced to confess. Finally, Salazar was unable to find any physical evidence of witchcraft, nor could he locate eyewitnesses to witchcraft who were not suspects themselves. His experiences gave him pause. Inquisitors were supposed to pay attention to intent, because heresy was purposeful, not accidental. They were supposed to conduct trials on the basis of evidence that could be perceived. They also were supposed to prefer witnesses "outside complicity," meaning people who were not accomplices to the errors under investigation. By the end of 1611, Salazar believed his tribunal's cases were insufficiently grounded in what should have been essential legal principles.[16]

In March 1612, Salazar sent a report to Madrid that outlined the weaknesses of his tribunal's prosecutions of witch suspects. Over the next two years, he and his two inquisitor colleagues argued about the quality and quantity of their proof. In 1614, the governing council of the Spanish Inquisition, called the Suprema, asked Salazar to come to Madrid to help hash out new rules for the Inquisition's witchcraft prosecutions. Salazar complied; once he and the Suprema had completed the revisions, the new guidelines were sent to every inquisition tribunal in the Spanish Empire.[17] Even more importantly, in 1614, the Suprema also nullified every witch investigation and trial conducted by the Logroño tribunal between 1609 and 1614. The Inquisition leadership lifted sentences of exile and imprisonment, restored the possessions of convicted witches, and explicitly reestablished the honor of the people who had been prosecuted for witchcraft over that five-year period.

It was extraordinary for the Spanish Inquisition to admit to error or rescind its own verdicts. The Zugarramurdi witch hunt—named after the village in which it began—consequently has become one of the most famous witchcraft episodes in European history. At the same time, historians have known for decades that we lack crucial documents about the persecution because Napoleon's troops burned

16. Historians have disagreed as to whether Salazar was originally and perpetually skeptical about the reality of witchcraft. For opposing views, see Henningsen, *Witches' Advocate*; and Homza, *Village Infernos*, 135–37, 153–58, 162–65, 172–75, 188–90.

17. For an analysis of the 1614 guidelines, see Homza, *Village Infernos*, 175–80.

down the Logroño tribunal when they invaded Spain in 1808. All the witches' trials were destroyed; the only inquisition evidence about the witch hunt that survives are letters and reports exchanged between Logroño and Madrid and preserved as copies.[18]

Yet it turns out that the other two legal jurisdictions in Navarre—embodied in the royal secular court and the bishop's court, both of which were in Pamplona—played unexpected and pivotal roles in this witch hunt, as their surviving records attest. Multiple secular prosecutions in Pamplona had this witch hunt as their foundation, though the trials formally were for slander, attempted homicide, and assault. People accused of being witches and tortured by neighbors filed lawsuits against their attackers and won. Parishioners who were tormented over witchcraft suspicions by their village priest underwrote a trial against that priest and won.[19] As Inquisitor Salazar moved through Navarre in 1611, he not only learned about these prosecutions in the other courts but also supported them. When he put the secular and episcopal prosecutions together with the eighty-one witchcraft confessions revoked in his and his employees' presence, he began to understand how confessions could have been fictitious, even though he was trained to regard confessions as the best possible proof. Salazar never doubted whether witches could be real. He never expressed misgivings about the institution that employed him. Instead, he came to radical conclusions through paying close attention to the details of legal testimony and the circumstances of confessions.

As Inquisitor Salazar started his visitation in May 1611, he soon went through Olague and spoke to some of the children and adults in this book, who referred to him in their legal testimony. Even more importantly, this book allows readers to see a witch hunt that was a youth-driven event. Sometimes, historians have posited that children's actions and emotions could have no appreciable impact on adults in European history, but the evidence from Olague proves otherwise.[20] At

---

18. For some of the surviving inquisitorial texts in translation, see Henningsen, *Salazar Documents*. The primary surviving Inquisition dossier, which is in the Archivo Histórico Nacional (AHN) in Madrid, can be accessed at http://pares.mcu.es /ParesBusquedas20/catalogo/show /2340978.

19. Homza, "When Witches Litigate"; Homza, *Village Infernos*, 141–46.

20. Maza, "Kids Aren't All Right."

the same time, scholars often have argued that witchcraft accusations were routine in this epoch.[21] The documents here illustrate instead how dysfunctional witch-hunting could be for communal and familial relationships.

The Olague texts also support modern scholarly findings that witches and their victims were never strangers.[22] The children and adults who accused neighbors, denied allegations, attacked and slandered each other, and inflicted and suffered public dishonor knew each other very well.[23] Like most sites in this witch persecution, Olague was tiny. Located twelve miles north of Pamplona, the village reported twenty-five heads of household in a census from 1606: if each household held on average five people, the total population would have come to 125.[24] As was the case throughout early modern Navarre, Olague's residents were generally illiterate and predominantly Basque-speaking. Most owned at least a few pigs, goats, sheep, cattle, or oxen. Though their wealth varied, they all could expect to be vulnerable to subsistence crises caused by drought, worm and beetle infestations, unseasonably cold temperatures, or plague. Hunger was predictable; infant mortality was routine.

Beyond these facts of life, Olague's residents shared a Catholic religious culture as well as the same honor code. Cultural imperatives about religion meant that people believed in the Devil and witches, though they could turn those beliefs in manipulative and hostile directions. Cultural expectations about marriage and honor meant that women in miserable unions had few options. Cultural expectations about honor and shame meant that when men and women were

21. Rojas, "Bad Christians and Hanging Toads"; Tausiet, *Urban Magic.*

22. Briggs, *Witches and Neighbors*; Roper, *Witch Craze*; Kivelson, "So That They Will Love Me"; Geschiere, "Witchcraft and the Dangers of Intimacy."

23. Such profound acquaintance begs the question of how lifelong neighbors could inflict so much

suffering on each other over witchcraft beliefs: Roper, *Witch Craze*, 2–5.

24. Olague was too small to support a notary: villagers instead must have gone to Pamplona to file legal documents. Because notaries in Pamplona were so numerous and notarial records in this epoch were so abundant, we have not yet been able to locate the notarial sources that would illuminate Olague's society and economy.

defamed as witches in public, they sometimes struck back in legal ways that they could not sustain financially, with disastrous consequences.

The calamity over witchcraft in Olague began in the spring of 1611 and conformed to the larger witch hunt's general patterns. Numerous youngsters asserted that they had become the Devil's servants; the cause of their transformation lay with neighbors and relatives who were witches themselves and had flown them through the air to meet the Devil and venerate him. Parents and relatives were enraged over the damage being done to their children, who told them what had occurred and announced they had been turned into child witches (niños embrujados) through their contact with the Devil. The children knew the adults they had seen at the Devil's gatherings. They consequently stormed around their village as a gang and shouted witchcraft accusations at others, allegations that they repeated since they were taken to the akelarres multiple times. The child witches' parents then confronted the witch suspects, first verbally, then physically.

The damage caused by Olague's child witches was substantial. The epithet of "witch" was a severe affront. Verbal slurs on the street, in church, or in any other open space crippled personal and familial honor, and this was true no matter the speaker, recipient, audience, or circumstances. An affront became that much more ruinous if it was reiterated. Having the wider community echo or talk about the slander, even if it was false, reinforced the injury.[25]

At the same time, children in early modern Navarre enjoyed a peculiar sort of legal immunity when it came to defamation.[26] When children spoke public insults, they could not be prosecuted for slander; the evidence also indicates that "witch" was by far the predominant public slur that children uttered.[27] Hence, children in Olague and across Navarre became the perfect accusers of witchcraft between

25. Berraondo Piudo, "La violencia interpersonal," 162. For the impact of compounded insults, see Taylor, *Honor and Violence*.

26. To the best of my knowledge, we do not have research findings on children and defamation from other Spanish locales, but I would presume the same legal immunity held.

27. Scott Taylor found an instance in which an adult paid a child to call a woman a whore: *Honor and Violence*, 183.

1608 and 1614. They could repeat one public allegation after another, and there was no legal mechanism to stop them.

Some adults in Olague lost their lives and had their houses burned down due to the children's accusations.[28] Ultimately, people fled. In July 1612, a census found that the village had twenty-six households, but practically one-third—eight—had missing owners.[29] We do not know if those families ever returned.

Chapter 1 presents inquisitorial correspondence and pamphlet literature about the witch hunt for the purposes of context. Chapters 2, 3, and 4 are devoted to three legal texts that only surfaced in 2014, 2018, and 2019, respectively, when archivists in Pamplona discovered them. Two of those documents are secular trials for slander against adults in Pamplona's Royal Court.[30] The third is a petition for a marital separation, filed in Pamplona's episcopal court by a wife against her husband.[31] None of these three legal cases was specifically for the crime or heresy of witchcraft, and none was conducted by the Spanish Inquisition; nevertheless, they were provoked by the larger witch hunt that the Inquisition was supervising.

The two slander cases excerpted and translated here offer an especially complicated legal trajectory. In a typical trial for any crime in the royal secular court, including defamation, defendants could present witnesses for their side. But in these slander prosecutions, the defendants went one step further and filed defamation lawsuits of their own against the adult plaintiffs who had insulted them. Thus, the defamation trials in chapters 2 and 3 involve two sides pursuing proof of slander, which means the legal records have more intricate bodies

---

28. See chaps. 2 and 3, as well as Homza, *Village Infernos*, 109–21.

29. Depopulation over this witch hunt was even more extreme for the village of Arraioz. In the summer of 1612, Arraioz had thirty-six houses, but twenty-seven owners had fled. Homza, *Village Infernos*, 182–83.

30. AGN, *Tribunales reales*, #330569 and #41366.

31. Archivo diocesano de Pamplona (ADP), C/1.232, n. 38.

of evidence than we usually see. The original plaintiffs called many child witches to substantiate that the defendants were truly witches: if that were the case, then the plaintiffs had spoken the truth, and no slander was in play. Concurrently, the defendants called different child witches who said their accusations had been false, at which point the defendants had been defamed by the original plaintiffs who had hurled insults on the bogus evidence of children.

The following list demonstrates how the two slander trials unfolded:

Step 1: Olague children publicly and repeatedly named particular adults as the witches who were taking them to the Devil's *akelarres.*

Step 2: Olague adults reiterated the children's slurs against the witch suspects and even physically assaulted them.

Step 3: When the adult witch suspects insulted in turn their adult accusers, those accusers immediately filed lawsuits in Pamplona for defamation.

Step 4: The adult witch suspects were thus brought to trial not on witchcraft but on slander charges. They, in turn, filed their own slander cases against the adults who had called them witches.

Step 5: Both sets of adults—plaintiffs and defendants—called Olague's child witches to testify. The plaintiffs hoped the child witches would verify that the defendants were witches. The defendants hoped the child witches would verify that their public accusations had been false and had come about through coercion.

It may surprise modern readers to learn that children as young as six not only gave evidence in secular trials in this epoch but also had their statements treated as agential, though they typically were not formally sworn to speak the truth. Still, children's legal testimony was always potentially contentious, and readers will see how both sides in the trials tried to work the children's ages to their advantage.

The witch crisis in Olague could also have a context of marital strife, as chapter 4 demonstrates. Readers will also encounter María de Alzate, a woman in her early fifties, in chapter 2, where she testifies about the public and false allegations of witchcraft directed at her by her own daughter, an adolescent girl named Marimartín. Alzate and others told the Royal Court why Marimartín had accused her mother: her father and especially her stepbrother had used death threats to push her into false allegations. Chapter 4 explores the background to this domestic drama, which was horrific. María de Alzate was married to Juan de Unciti, who was Olague's blacksmith. Alzate and Unciti were second spouses for each other; their only child together was Marimartín, though both had offspring from their prior marriages. Unciti detested Alzate and abused her for years before taking advantage of the witch panic to try to ruin her through false accusations of witchcraft. The documentary basis of chapter 4 is a petition that Alzate filed in episcopal court in December 1611, seeking a marital separation from Unciti on the grounds that he was liable to kill her if she was forced to continue living with him. She won her legal case, though she may well have died of poverty afterward. Putting together the two slander cases and the petition for a marital separation allows us to see how witch-hunting, domestic viciousness, and gender norms could intersect.

For chapters 2, 3, and 4, it is important to understand that legal cases opened with statements and evidence for the plaintiff, before being followed by statements and evidence for the defendant. Both the plaintiff and the defendant had lawyers; both created what we call "interrogatories," which were lists of questions to put to certain witnesses. If witnesses were of sufficient age, they deposed under oath; later, they would be obliged to ratify their original statements under oath, and in the ratification process, they could alter what they had originally said.

Significantly, the majority, if not all, of the plaintiffs, defendants, and witnesses in these legal manuscripts were deposing in Basque.[32] Their statements under oath were translated into Spanish, which was the formal language of the three legal jurisdictions in Navarre. Modern historians have frequently cautioned us not to view legal statements as

---

32. For the predominance of Basque speakers in early modern Navarre, see Monteano Sorbet, *El iceberg Navarro.*

transmitting the true voices of our historical subjects.[33] People were responding to direct questions; their responses were confined in legal formulas.[34] With the Basque-to-Spanish translations in play here, that warning seems even more appropriate. Yet people testifying in these prosecutions were not confined to what interrogators wanted or expected to hear.[35] Deponents could decline to answer questions and were not penalized for doing so. They could decide how much they wanted to say and make changes to their statements.[36] Such conditions held true whether children or adults were testifying.

33. German historians of witchcraft, whose surviving sources very often were produced under torture, can be adamant that the witch's "voice" cannot be detected: Voltmer, "Witch in the Courtroom." The extant sources from this witch hunt were not produced under such conditions.

34. For a classic caution about historians' use of legal sources, see Kuehn, "Reading Microhistory."

35. As an example, see chapter 4, where Juan de Unciti calls defense witnesses who verify his domestic abuse instead.

36. For a thoughtful evaluation of hearing subaltern voices in inquisitorial settings, see García-Arenal, "Polyphony of Voices."

CHAPTER 1

Prior Events

This chapter contains documents that provide a wider context for events in Olague. The first text is the first letter that inquisitors in Logroño wrote to their superiors in Madrid about the witches, dated February 1609. Next, readers will encounter two confessions to witchcraft made by a teenager and a child in December 1609 to an inquisitor who was on visitation in Navarre: these young people revoked their confessions two years later. Fourth in sequence are excerpts from a published pamphlet on the witches, whose content relied on the judicial sentences read aloud at the Inquisition's *auto de fe* in November 1610. Last, we have two letters from an inquisition commissioner, Leon de Araníbar, which he wrote in January and February 1611 to Logroño's inquisitors. Inquisition commissioners were generally priests; their work for the Inquisition consisted of taking down witness testimony before sending it to the tribunal. While Araníbar and his inquisitor employers expected the 1610 *auto de fe* to quell witchcraft accusations, Navarre's villages continued to swarm with suspicions, denunciations, and popular violence. Though Araníbar lamented the possibility of vigilantism in his letters in early 1611, he had been encouraging villagers to force witch suspects into confessions.[1]

IMPORTANT CHARACTERS, IN ORDER OF APPEARANCE

Juan de Becerra Holguín, inquisitor in Logroño[2]
Juan de Valle Alvarado, inquisitor in Logroño[3]

---

1. Homza, *Village Infernos*, 44–46, Homza, "When Witches Litigate," 269.
2. For his career, see Homza, *Village Infernos*, 188.

3. For his career, see Homza, *Village Infernos*, 188.

Gracia de Lizarraga, confessed teenage witch

Catalina de Antoco, the adult witch who took Gracia de Lizarraga
to the *akelarres*

Juan de Picabea, confessed child witch

Margarita de Viscancho, who took Juan de Picabea to the *akelarres*

Juan de Mongastón, printer in Pamplona who published an
account in January 1611 of the Inquisition's *auto de fe* in 1610

María de Suretegui, one of the first witches in the village of
Zugarramurdi, who was penanced in the *auto de fe* to six
months of exile

Miguel de Goiburu, a male witch from Zugarramurdi, who
was reconciled to the Catholic Church in effigy during the
November 1610 *auto de fe*[4] and died in the inquisition prison
in autumn 1609

Leon de Araníbar, inquisition commissioner and abbot of the Pre-
monstratensian monastery in Urdax, which held seigneurial
rights over Zugarramurdi

Graciana de Barrenechea, an older, alleged "master witch" of the
village of Arraioz (though Araníbar did not specify as much,
Barrenechea died while in the custody of another inquisition
employee, the notary Miguel de Narbarte)[5]

LETTER FROM INQUISITORS JUAN DE BECERRA AND
JUAN DE VALLE ALVARADO TO THE SUPREMA IN MADRID,
FEBRUARY 3, 1609

On January 12 of this year, we received a report that will go with this
letter, which relayed information about a great complicity of male
and female witches, all residents of the village of Zugarramurdi in
Navarre.[6] . . . We have seen from the report that the foundation of

4. For charts of those sentenced
by the Inquisition in November 1610,
see Henningsen, *Witches' Advocate*,
145–48, 198–200.

5. Homza, "When Witches
Litigate," 261–64. Barrenechea was
tortured in Narbarte's home; although

Narbarte was not there when she died,
his daughters were. In 1612, a prosecutor from the secular court in Pamplona
attempted to have Narbarte charged
with Barrenechea's murder.

6. This source comes from AHN,
Inqu., Leg. 1679, images 219–20.

that sect is apostasy from our holy Catholic faith and adoration of the Devil.[7] And we have seen what was ordered by Your Lordship [the Suprema] in similar cases of the witches' sect, which were presented in this inquisition tribunal in 1526 . . . and 1555. We have also seen the instructions that Your Lordship sent about those cases, which were intended to verify and find out the truth about this sect, on account of the doubt that then was in play, that all of it could have been dreams.[8]

. . . Considering what a large number of people are now involved in the sect, who have confessed or been testified against, we think they cannot be arrested without a great deal of scandal.[9] . . . It seemed to us that what was most advisable was to bring [here] four of the people who confessed to being witches, and who have the greatest number of witnesses against them. In this tribunal, they were interrogated and cross-examined in the most suitable way in order to verify the aim [behind the sect]. . . . The four witches were put into the tribunal's secret jails, so that the first hearings with them could be held. . . .

Before the first four hearings were finished, Graciana de Iriart— the head and master of this witch complicity—with two of her sons and three other men, her sons-in-law, . . . came to this tribunal of their own volition.[10] . . . All of them [had] confessed before the vicar

7. The inquisitors believed that the witch suspects were engaging in heresy and not simply harmful magic. Harmful magic was under the purview of the secular legal jurisdiction, although inquisitors viewed that evidence as compounding the witches' offense of heresy.

8. Here, Inquisitors Becerra and Valle were taking some legal precedents seriously while discounting others. By insisting that the witches of Zugarramurdi were truly flying, they were brushing off the canon *Episcopi*, an authoritative text of medieval church law. The canon *Episcopi* dates from the tenth century, though medieval and early modern Europeans believed it had been issued at the Council of Ancyra in 314 CE; its purported antiquity gave it additional weight. The *Episcopi* stated that women who believed they could fly through the air with the goddess

Diana were deluded by demons. Catholic theologians and inquisitors in this time period consequently had to at least entertain the possibility that witches were dreaming, though they could counterbalance the *Episcopi* with Christian New Testament accounts of the Devil carrying Jesus through the air.

9. "Scandal" (*escándalo*) in early modern Spain signified disorder and tumult. The inquisitors feared that too many arrests would agitate the village of Zugarramurdi. Though they neglected to say so here, their prison was small and dilapidated and could not hold large numbers of people awaiting trial.

10. The inquisitors identified Graciana de Iriart by her husband's surname. She was eighty years old when she appeared in the tribunal; she died in the inquisition jail in September 1609. Henningsen, *Witches' Advocate*, 145.

of Zugarramurdi and residents there that they were witches and had separated themselves from our holy Catholic faith. . . . It was ordered in the tribunal that each one should individually enter the courtroom, upon which each of them, with the same reasoning and vocabulary, said that . . . the justice of that land [Zugarramurdi] was proceeding against them, and wanted to carry out great punishments upon them because they had confessed that they were witches before the vicar and other people, when they really were not. They had falsely testified. If they had said and confessed that they were witches, it was because people [in the village] had seriously squeezed and threatened them if they did not confess. Each of the six said this with the same words.[11] Finally, we ordered a man from Zugarramurdi to enter the courtroom, who had been paid by the six to act as their guide to this city. When we asked him what justice system was proceeding against these six persons or anyone else in Zugarramurdi, he said that there was no justice or any person proceeding against the six.[12] He had never seen or understood such a thing. He only knew that four residents of Zugarramurdi had been brought to this tribunal as prisoners. . . .

Thus we think that through some consultation or counsel from the Devil (with whom Graciana de Iriart is on most familiar terms), or from their relatives, the six have presented themselves in this inquisition tribunal to exempt themselves from the witchcraft confessions that they made before the vicar and other people . . . and to imply that they are not guilty.

The letter ends with a statement that the inquisitors have voted to imprison the six new suspects from Zugarramurdi.

11. The inquisitors suspected the six were lying because the latter supposedly used identical language as they described their situation. The witch suspects were deposing in Basque, which the inquisitors did not understand: they had to rely on translators. What we do not know is whether the translators made the suspects' speech uniform.

12. Here too the language issue could have obstructed the inquisitors' understanding. When they referred to a "justice of that land," they undoubtedly meant a secular legal officer of some sort. No secular justice proceeded against the first witch suspects in Zugarramurdi; instead, they were victims of community pressure, a circumstance that inquisitors in this persecution did not grasp until the middle of 1611.

A CONFESSION TO WITCHCRAFT BEFORE INQUISITOR
JUAN DE VALLE ALVARADO, WHILE HE WAS ON VISITATION
IN NAVARRE IN DECEMBER 1609

In the village of Tolosa, December 13, 1609, in the afternoon hearing with Juan de Barrenechea, Basque interpreter, a familiar and a notary of the Inquisition, and a resident of Tolosa.[13] A girl appeared on her own volition, and swore in the necessary legal way to tell the truth and to preserve secrecy.[14] She said her name was Gracia de Lizarraga; she is the daughter of Sabas de Lizarraga, coal merchant, and his wife, Maricho de Ubiría, residents of the village of Lesaka. She is seventeen years old. To discharge her conscience, she comes to confess how perhaps ten years ago, when she was in bed asleep with a brother of hers (and she does not recall what time of day it was), Catalina de Antoco went to that bed, and took her out of the house through a little window. In an instant, Catalina took her to a field that is next to the Hermitage of Piety, and this witness found herself there dressed and awake, . . . and it seemed that Catalina had carried her in the air. In that field, there was a large black thing in the shape of a goat, with the face of an ugly and frightening man, with horns on its head and claws on its feet and hands, seated with great majesty on a chair.[15]

Before the Goat, there were many female and male witches, dancing and leaping with a lot of noise, to the sounds of tambourines and pipes.[16] Catalina took this witness before that evil Goat whom they called lord, and told the Goat how she had brought this witness for his service, and he thanked her. Catalina put this witness with other children who were set away from the witches, guarding some toads that were dressed in colored clothing and wearing bells. Catalina gave

13. AHN, Inqu., Leg. 1679, images 897–901. "Familiars" were men hired by Spanish inquisitors to assist them with their work. Familiars were not authorized to take down witness testimony, but the fact that Juan de Barrenechea was also a notary meant that he could have assisted with writing legal documents.

14. At seventeen, Gracia was old enough to take a formal oath to tell the truth. Anyone who deposed before the Spanish Inquisition had to promise to maintain secrecy as to what they might say and hear in the tribunal, though they certainly did not necessarily do so.

15. The Devil in Navarre typically appeared as a goat.

16. Historians have noted how often village rituals such as dancing became integrated into accounts of the Devil's sabbat. Roper, *Witch Craze*, 111; Briggs, *Witches and Neighbors*, 40.

this witness a little bar and ordered her to guard the toads. After a long time, Catalina returned this witness to her bed through the same window, carrying her through the air with great speed. And this witness immediately slept and did not awaken until the next day. From that moment on, Catalina continually carried this witness in the air in the same way, and they went to the witches' *akelarres* three times a week, usually Mondays, Wednesdays, and Fridays.[17] They also went to the *akelarres* on the nights of the main Catholic feast days.

At the *akelarres*, there were also some flames—without firewood—and the older witches moved through the flames and said they were not burned, . . . and she does not know how, but her parents and other family members never missed her while she was at the *akelarres*. She does not know if Catalina anointed her with something to carry her to the *akelarres*, because when Catalina took her, she was always asleep.[18] . . . Seven years ago, more or less, Catalina took this witness one night to that evil lord [the Devil], and with threats, she made her renounce God, our Lord [Jesus], and his mother, the Virgin Mary, and all the saints, baptism, confirmation, chrism, and her parents and godparents. [And then] the Devil gave Catalina some money. From that moment forward, this witness held the Goat as her god and believed he would save her. She thought the Goat was better than the true god of the Christians. She believed these things at night in the *akelarres*, as well as during the day when she was away from them, no matter when it was.[19]

The Devil had her so blinded that she did not consider her error until eight days ago, when she saw the tumult and racket that was occurring in the village of Lesaka over the matter of witches.[20] Then she began to consider carefully what she had done by renouncing God, . . . and suddenly she saw how she was deceived and the evil state she

17. Three is a sacred number in Christianity because it refers to the Trinity, the threefold divinity of Father, Son, and Holy Spirit. Here, the number was being turned toward the diabolical.

18. The notion that the child-witches were sleeping helped substantiate their status as victims.

19. From Gracia's standpoint, this detail proved that she had not been dreaming.

20. In the Christian New Testament, John 8:44, the Devil is called a liar and the father of lies. It was common in this witch hunt for suspects to describe themselves as deceived or blinded by the Devil and his followers.

was in, and she saw that the Goat was not god nor could he be god, but rather the Devil who wanted to carry her to Hell. . . . She begged God to forgive her, and the Inquisition to treat her mercifully.

Gracia de Lizarraga revoked her December 1609 confession to witchcraft in August 1611. In 1609, many of her neighbors in Lesaka had told her that she was a witch and had the sign of being one in her left eye. Witchcraft in Navarre could entail both a sign in the left eye, often in the shape of a toad, and a Devil's mark, which often was made on the left shoulder.

ANOTHER CONFESSION TO WITCHCRAFT BEFORE INQUISITOR JUAN DE VALLE ALVARADO, WHILE HE WAS ON VISITATION IN DECEMBER 1609

In the village of Tolosa on December 13, 1609, in the afternoon hearing . . . with Juan de Barrenechea, Basque interpreter, a familiar of the Inquisition in this village and a notary of it.[21] A boy appeared of his own volition, and because he was so young, he did not swear an oath, but he promised to tell the truth and to observe secrecy. He said he was named Juan de Picabea, son of Juan de Picabea, coal merchant, and María de Ochogorría, residents of the village of Lesaka. He is eleven years old. He comes to confess that he has been a witch since he was a baby; he does not know, cannot recall, and cannot know who took him to the *akelarre* during the time that he [was so young]. . . . After he possessed understanding and awareness, he remembers that he was always taken three nights a week, Mondays, Wednesdays, and Fridays, at night, by Margarita de Viscancho, the widow.[22] She took him while he was sleeping in bed with his parents and other people. She took him through a window.[23] She carried him to a field that is next

21. AHN, Inqu., Leg. 1679, images 881–87.

22. Older, menopausal women were often imagined as witches in early modern Europe. Roper, *Witch Craze*, chap. 7. Still, witch suspects in this persecution were of all ages, including women who were pregnant or who had just given birth. Men were imagined as witches in Navarre as well.

23. Juan may well have been responding to direct questions from Inquisitor Valle as to how, exactly, he went to the *akelarres*.

to the Hermitage of Our Lady of Piety. Other times, she took him to the field of Lauburo. In that field, the Devil was there in the shape of a goat, with horns on his head and claws on his feet and hands, with a face like a man, though a terrifying and horrible one. The Goat was seated on a golden chair with great majesty. Before him, there was a large number of men and women, dancing to music.

As soon as he had the use of reason, Margarita told him not to say the name of Jesus [in the *akelarre*]. She told him to guard dressed toads that wore bells. When she gave him a little bar [to guard them], the toads complained and the older witches put him to bed. There was a brightness in the *akelarres* with which people there could see everything happening, and he did not know what that brightness was. There also were some flames, through which the witches leaped. They threw themselves into the flames many times and were not burned.

Some nights, there were tables in the *akelarres* without table-cloths, but with foods that the witches ate. Sometimes, he would go to the table to eat, [but when] he extended his hand, he did not find what he wanted to take.[24] Some nights, the older witches would skin toads and put them into a large pot. . . . He did not know what they did with the contents of the pot, because he and the other little witches did not come to the place where the witches were working, nor were they allowed to come, because the older witches would whip them.[25]

This witness also saw how the Devil sometimes separated out the women and then took on the appearance of a tall and graceful man. Sometimes the Devil took on the appearance of a beautiful woman, but this witness did not see the male witches deal with him.[26]

24. The idea of a banquet of food that disappears was a common feature for the sabbat. It speaks to the Devil's propensity to deceive, as well as the subsistence crises of early modern Europe. Briggs, *Witches and Neighbors*, 49.

25. The implication was that the witches were using toads to make poisons for harmful magic.

26. One convention in this persecution was that the Devil had sex with his female and male followers during their gatherings. Juan de Picabea was suggesting that the Devil changed into an incubus or succubus by taking on male or female form. Other child witches did not mention shape-shifting where the Devil and his sexual partners were concerned.

Juan went on to relay how Margarita had forced him to renounce Christianity. Like the older Gracia, Juan too had a moment of spiritual revelation, fifteen days before confessing to Inquisitor Valle Alvarado. Juan noted that the Devil had wanted to deceive him and carry him to hell, and he "begged God to pardon him, and begged the Holy Inquisition to admit him to the union and flock of the Holy Catholic faith and the church of Rome." In August 1611, he revoked his earlier witchcraft confession. In 1609, many people in Lesaka had told eleven-year-old Juan that he was a witch and had the sign of being one in his eye.

A PRINTED ACCOUNT OF THE WITCHES WHO APPEARED
IN THE *AUTO DE FE* THAT THE INQUISITORS CELEBRATED
IN THE CITY OF LOGROÑO ON NOVEMBER 7 AND 8, 1610,
AND THE THINGS AND CRIMES FOR WHICH THEY WERE
PUNISHED[27]

Printer Juan de Mongastón to the reader

This account came into my hands, and because it is so substantial, and contains the most important points of the legal sentences of the people who were . . . condemned for belonging to the diabolical sect of witches, I wanted to print it [in Spanish], so that everyone can take notice of the great evils that are committed in that sect. May it serve as a warning as to the care with which every Christian must watch over his house and family.

The pamphlet

. . . Once the new witch renounces [the Christian faith], the Devil says that henceforth, the witch will not believe in the god of the Christians but rather in the Devil, because the Devil is the true god and lord who will save the witch and take her to Paradise. . . . The Devil uses his

---

27. This pamphlet, printed by Juan de Mongastón, is available in a modern edition. See Fernández Nieto, *Proceso a la brujería*, 30–72.

left hand to mark the witch, and lowering his head toward the witch's left shoulder (or other parts of the body, depending on his wishes) he makes a mark in the witch's flesh with one of his nails. The marking hurts and draws blood, and the Devil catches the blood in a cloth or a little glass, and the novice witch feels great pain from this injury, which lasts more than a month, and the mark lasts for the rest of the witch's life. Afterward, the Devil makes a mark (which does not hurt) in the pupil of the witch's eye, in the shape of a little toad, which is the sign that allows the witches to recognize each other.[28] . . .

After the new witch has renounced Christianity, the Devil and the other older witches tell the novice not to say the name of Jesus or the Virgin Mary, and not to make the sign of the Cross; then, they order the novice to go rest and dance with the other witches who are around the fake fires that the Devil creates there.[29] The Devil tells the witches that these are the fires of Hell and to go in and out of them, and they will see how the flames do not burn or cause any pain at all, but rather are enjoyable and fun. The witches should not be afraid to do all the evil they can, since the fires of Hell do not burn or injure them in any way. . . .

It is an established fact, confessed by all the witches, that as soon as they became witches, they stopped being able to see the most holy sacrament of the altar, the Eucharist. . . .

When the French girl [María de Ximildegui] returned to Zugarramurdi, where she was raised, she told the village that she had been

28. In earlier episodes of witchcraft in Navarre, witch finders, who could be children, claimed to see marks in the pupils of witches' eyes. For example, in 1595, in the village of Intza, the witch finder was an adolescent female who attributed her powers to having had a witch for a mother. In the Navarrese persecution of 1608–14, there are occasional mentions of witch finders, but we have been unable to discover much about them.

29. Pronouncing the name of Jesus or Mary at the *akelarres* caused the Devil to disappear and the witches to disburse.

30. Ximildegui had been working across the border in the French Basque region of the Pays de Labourd, where the judge and demonologist Pierre de Lancre and his colleague Jean d'Espaignet would investigate claims of witchcraft in 1609. Rolley and Machielsen, "Mythmaker of the Sabbat." It appears that Ximildegui was never prosecuted by the Spanish Inquisition for witchcraft, though she was examined by Inquisitor Valle Alvarado in Zugarramurdi when he was on visitation in 1609.

a witch in France.[30] Though she was now free of that wicked sect, she said there was a sect in Zugarramurdi too, and she previously had gone to its *akelarre* two or three times. The French girl [said that] certain persons in Zugarramurdi were witches, among them, María de Suretegui.[31] When María's husband got wind of this rumor, he and his relatives demanded a duel over it. With loud cries and anger, María insisted she was not a witch, and it was a great wickedness and false testimony to say that she had carried away the French girl to the *akelarre*. With great screams, she demanded vengeance from her husband against the French girl, . . . and the French girl responded, "put me in front of her, and I will convince her and make her confess the truth. . . ."

Taking the French girl to María's house, and putting them face to face, the French girl stated all the things that had gone on in the *akelarre*, and María defended herself, swearing none of it was true. [But] the French girl knew so much to say that everyone was persuaded into believing that it *was* true, and they pressured María to confess. Seeing herself cut off and convicted, María broke into a sweat; a great anxiety came over her, and she fell, swooning, from her seat. It looked as if she had something caught in her throat, which prevented her from speaking the truth.[32] Turning on the ground with a great sigh, a terrible-smelling breath came from her mouth, and then she confessed that what the French girl said was true, and that she had been a witch since she was very little, through instruction from her aunt, María Chipía [de Barrenechea] (who was reconciled at the *auto de fe*).[33] She relayed many things that she had done while she was a witch, which is why her husband and neighbors then took her to the

31. Suretegui was convicted of witchcraft by the Spanish Inquisition in 1610, but her spiritual combat against the Devil made an impression on the inquisitors, who removed her *sambenito* at their *auto de fe* in 1610: Homza, *Village Infernos*, 63. She was reconciled to the church and given a penance of six months' exile. Henningsen, *Witches' Advocate*, 198.

32. Later in the persecution, witch suspects told inquisitors that the Devil was strangling them to prevent them from speaking the truth.

33. The foul-smelling breath of María Suretegui echoes the evil-smelling breath of the Devil as he received supplicants in the *akelarre*. María Chipía de Barrenechea, age fifty-two, was reconciled to the church with life imprisonment at the *auto de fe*: Henningsen, *Witches' Advocate*, 199.

vicar of Zugarramurdi to confess. With her having confessed, the vicar counseled her to beg pardon from the village's residents for the evils she had committed, and she publicly confessed and begged their pardon.[34] As soon as she confessed, she began to see the consecrated Host in the Mass. Never up to that point had she been able to see the Host, because she started to be a witch when she was very small.

The Devil was greatly aware of the evils that had to result from María de Suretegui's confession. He told his witches how furious he was that María had left his banner: then, they began to pursue her and go to her house at night, to drag her out and carry her to the *akelarre*, frightening and threatening her if she did not go.[35] . . . The Devil and the witches found María de Suretegui in the kitchen, surrounded by many people whom she had asked to come, to accompany and guard her . . . because she had told them that the *akelarre* was happening that night, and the witches would come to mistreat her. The Devil and . . . the witches put themselves behind a bench, and over the back of it, they looked to see where María was and what she was doing, and they began to call her with certain signs, so that she would go with them. And María Chipía [de Barrenechea], her master and aunt, along with another of her sisters, put themselves into the chimney shaft, and from there, they called her with their hands, making signs that she should go with them, and they threatened her, putting their fingers to their foreheads, and swearing that if she did not go with them, she would pay.[36]

María de Suretegui defended herself, screaming and pointing out where the witches were, but the other people in the house could

34. It is telling that Zugarramurdi's villagers did not automatically take Suretegui to the inquisitors in Logroño. Surviving texts from this witch hunt demonstrate repeatedly that accused witches were expected to confess their crimes and heresy to their local priests and then to beg public pardon from their neighbors.

35. The word for "banner" here is literally *banda*, meaning "flag." The Devil and his crew were imagined as an army.

36. The concept that witchcraft ran in families was always present in Navarre, and it certainly can be seen in the earliest stages of this particular witch hunt, when many members of the same families were accused. Nevertheless, one of the striking aspects of this witch hunt was how many purported witches lacked family reputations as such. See chapter 3, as well as Rowlands, "Gender, Ungodly Parents and a Witch Family."

not see them, because the Devil had enchanted them and thrown shadows over them so that only María could see the witches. María said, screaming, "Leave me, traitors, do not pursue me anymore, I am so fed up for having followed the Devil." And seeing how much they were pressuring her to go with them, María took out a rosary that she wore at her throat, and raising the cross of it up high, said, "Leave me, leave me, I do not want to serve the Devil anymore. This cross is what I want, and this cross must defend me."[37]

By making the sign of the cross upon herself, and speaking the name of Jesus and the Holy Virgin Mary, she got the witches to disappear, and all of them went to the roof of the house where the tiles were, making a loud noise. . . . To take vengeance upon her, the witches ripped up the cabbages of the garden, and they broke and destroyed many apple trees. . . .

All the younger witches cannot go to the *akelarre* if they are not in the company of their masters, who go to their houses every night, and anoint them and carry them away.[38] The older witches take care to return the younger ones to their beds. The witches who have formally renounced their Christianity own the dressed toads, and they feed and sustain them, . . . and these dressed toads are demons in the shape of toads, and they accompany and help the witches to commit ever-greater evils. . . . The witches have to feed the toads: they give them bread, wine, and other things for their sustenance; and the toads eat by raising the food to their mouths with their hands. If the witches don't give them anything, the toads say, "Our friend, give me a little gift, give me something to eat." The witches frequently talk with the toads and tell them things, and the Devil pays great attention to the care with which the witches treat the toads, and he punishes them severely when they have been negligent in feeding them.

. . . On the evenings of the major Christian feast days—Easter, Epiphany, the Ascension, Corpus Christi, All Saints, Purification of the Virgin Mary, the Assumption and Birth of Our Lady, and the night of St. John the Baptist—the witches gather at the *akelarre* to perform a

---

37. The sense of spiritual combat is palpable in this account. The idea of battle against the Devil recurs constantly in the surviving sources: Homza, *Village Infernos*, chap. 2.

38. A "master" witch could be male or female.

solemn adoration of the Devil. They all confess with him, and accuse themselves of sins—such as how often they entered the church, how many Masses they heard, and all the other things they might have done as Christians—as well as the evils they could have done but failed to do.[39] And the Devil seriously reprimands them and tells them they must not do any Christian act.

Then, the Devil's servants, who are other devils, though smaller, erect an altar with a black cloth, which is old, ugly, and faded, and they put on it some statues of diabolical figures, along with the chalice, host, missal, and cruet, and some clothes like the ones they use to say Mass in churches, although these are black, ugly, and dirty. Helped by his servants, the Devil puts on the clothes, and then they all officiate at Mass, with low, hoarse, and tuneless voices. And the Devil sings from a book like a missal, but it looks as if it is made of stone. He also preaches a sermon, in which he says his congregation should not be arrogant and want other gods, because he is the one who will save them and take them to Paradise. Even if they undergo hardship and toils in this life, he will give them much rest in the next one. And they should commit as much evil as they can against Christians. . . .

On the night of St. John's Day, after his Mass is finished, the Devil goes with all the witches to the church, and opening the doors, the Devil stays outside while the witches commit many offenses and insults against the Holy Cross and the statues of the saints.

. . . [Male witch] Miguel de Goiburu relates that at certain times of the year, he and the oldest female witches create an offering for the Devil that greatly pleases him.[40] To do it, Goiburu and the witches go at night to church, and each one carries a basket with a handle, and they dig up the bodies of the dead who have already wasted away.[41] From those bodies, they remove the bones of the toes, the cartilage

39. A reversal of the Lord's Prayer, in which Christians beg forgiveness for sins.

40. Goiburu confessed to witchcraft before the inquisitors in Logroño. He died in the fall of 1609 and was reconciled to the church in effigy at the November 1610 *auto de fe*. Henningsen, *Witches' Advocate*, 145, 198.

41. Witches in Europe were presumed to kill and even eat infants, but their consumption of adults in this persecution was unique in European history. Though not mentioned in this excerpt, these witches also allegedly practiced vampirism by putting needles up the noses or anuses of sleeping infants to suck their blood.

from the noses, and all those small bones that the corpses have, and the putrid brains (although these parts are being consumed by the earth, they take a long time to disappear). The witches put the bones, cartilage, and brains in the baskets, and they cover up the graves with earth. And they carry a light in order to do all of this. . . . And [male witch] Juan de Etxalar states that when the witches go alone to do these things, without the Devil, the light they carry is a torch made from the arm of a child who died without being baptized—the whole arm—and they light the part where the fingers are, and it gives off light as if it were a torch.[42]

[When the witches reach the *akelarre* with the baskets,] the Devil is very pleased with them. . . . And he takes the small baskets and empties them into a much larger one made of hemp, which is next to him, . . . and the Devil eats the bones, cartilage, and brains with his teeth, which are very large, and as white as those of Black people; and he eats in a gross way, clicking like a pig.[43] Asked why the Devil eats those bones, the witches said he did it to encourage and oblige them to eat them as well. So he gave the bones to the witches, and even though they [the bones] were very hard, the witches ate them easily, because the Devil gave them the grace and strength to enable them to chew and eat them. . . . And even though the brains were so disgusting, the witches ate them to make the Devil happy. . . .

LETTER FROM INQUISITION COMMISSIONER LEON DE ARANÍBAR IN ELIZONDO TO THE LOGROÑO INQUISITION TRIBUNAL, JANUARY 29, 1611[44]

After seeing the letter this month from Your Lordship, I carried out the task that the letter ordered me to do regarding the two women

---

42. Juan de Etxalar is identified by Henningsen as Juanes de Yribarren: *Witches' Advocate*, 155–56, 199. He was reconciled to the church, sentenced to one year of imprisonment, and exiled for life at the 1610 *auto de fe*.

43. Aside from the usual convention of the Devil as black in color, this is the only other detail that I have found in these sources that explicitly links the Devil to Black African populations. Far more commonly, the surviving materials link the Devil and witches to Jews. Homza, *Village Infernos*, 161–62.

44. AHN, Inqu., Leg. 1679, images 171–76, excerpted.

from Donoztebe-Santesteban. . . . The aforementioned two women are prisoners, [but there is] a great deal of anger from other places in the region, after seeing that these two were taken [prisoner], but so many others are left in place who do much more damage, given that they take babies every night to the *akelarres*. Carrying away the children is causing so much anger and unrest in the community that these very places have started to imprison, without authorization, the people who are carrying away the children. After I interfered in this, some became upset with me, telling me, what is this, that they and their local constables cannot imprison the male and female witches who take their children to their sect and make the children reject God, and whip and mistreat them, given that this wickedness is so publicly known and these traitors continue in it.

Having told them that the imprisonments are doing little good— since despite being imprisoned, the witch suspects continue to carry away the children—the villagers respond that it is good for the witches to suffer. They say they have experimented [and realized] that when the witches are [locked away] alone, they only snatch the children whom they carried away before, not the children who are still uninfected. And in order for the witches not to do more damage than they have already done, it is good that they be imprisoned.

The work [here] is great, and so are the racket and turmoil of the common people, and I am not enough [to quell it]. I attest to Your Lordship that I dare not leave the house so as not to hear the cries, feelings, and complaints of the common people. Even when I am in the house, they give me enough grief, because due to the position that Your Lordship has given me, they think I have more authority and jurisdiction than I actually possess.[45] May the divine majesty [of God] grant that we may see here someone from Your Lordship's tribunal, who is so desired by me and so important for the tranquility of these lands and the salvation of souls.[46]

45. In 1612, when Araníbar deposed in secular court in Pamplona, he said he encouraged villagers to force suspects into confessions because that was the only strategy that seemed to calm

parents down. AGN, *Tribunales reales* #072902, fol. 191r.

46. Araníbar is obliquely asking that one of the inquisitors in Logroño come to Navarre on visitation.

With this letter, I am sending Your Lordship the report regarding the witches [sic] the female witches of Arraioz, where, among others, the one most testified against as a witch, and the one who has carried away more children, is Graciana de Barrenechea, the most traitorous and obstinate [witch] I have seen in my life. Sometimes she was variable and confessed something, more out of compliance than for the remedy of her soul. Then, she would deny as much as she had said. One day, she seemed to be very contrite, due to the persuasion of her own daughter and son-in-law, and she publicly came to confess that she was a very famous witch. She begged pardon from her own daughter and son-in-law for having bewitched four or five [of their] children, all of whom have now confessed. And with [Graciana's] good persuasions, she was the reason that one of her granddaughters of marriageable age, named Chipitoa, confessed to this complicity. . . .

[Yet] just three or four days after this happened, the Devil did so much with Graciana (or through the counsel of Beatríz, wife of Gastón the stonemason, as is suspected) that she returned to denying as much as she had confessed. She said that she never had been a witch, nor did she know anything about it, and everything she had confessed was a lie, and she had gravely offended God in it. Since she was the one who did the greatest damage, the commotion of the place and the turmoil of the parents of children infected by her were so great that they imprisoned her without authorization. They tied her to a post by her arms in a house, and exhorted her to confess the truth.[47] Not having any solution with her, they left her alone in the way that I have described; after a quarter of an hour, they returned to examine her and found her unconscious. And they gave her up for dead, and sent a man to ask me if they could bury her in holy ground, because many of them wanted to throw her into the river. Then came the shouting of the women that she "should speak the blessed name of Jesus," but she never said it, and remained mute. Even though they wanted to put a blessed candle in her hands, she would not grab it, and they think she easily could have done so. Finally she exhaled, and being in her

47. In fact, the villagers took her to the house of Miguel de Narbarte, royal notary and inquisition familiar, where she was tortured and died.

death agony, a confessed girl-witch who was there began to scream, saying that she saw a Black man next to her [Graciana], something that no one else saw.[48] . . .

Accompanying this letter is the report on the valley of Ibargoyara, where the villages of Donamaria and Gaztelu are located. I have left many confessed child witches out of the report beyond the ones who are in it. Migueltxo de Micheltorena is very much testified against, not only by the confessed persons in the report, but also by many others. I have done as much as I could with him through good words, but he is so devoted to the Devil that halfway through confessing his crime, he told me he did not expect a remedy. I did what I could so that he would trust the mercy of God and Your Lordship, but it was all lost work. He will do much harm in carrying away children. Two old women are also carrying children away—Magdalen Moxo and the wife of Enekorena de Gaztelu—and certain others.

Also accompanying this letter is the report on the village of Oronoz. . . . I hope more will be discovered in a few days. There is not a corner in which there is not much to investigate; it seems impossible that this work can be finished in a thousand years. In the depositions that I am entering, I am leaving off specifying many children in order to avoid excessive length. It seems to me that [those children] are irrelevant now, because there are so many of them and they are very publicly known, and every day more are being discovered with great publicity. . . .

Some confessions of elderly people, who have been witches for many years, run short in terms of length, but not for lack of putting questions to them. I am asking about events and relationships that we know they carry out in the *akelarres*, but they respond that they do not know. It is not as if they arrive in a contrite state or with any [spiritual] pain, but only to comply with temporal justice and out of fear of the same, since they have been publicly testified against. For

---

48. Graciana de Barrenechea's sister and granddaughter confessed to witchcraft in December 1610 and then revoked those confessions in August 1611: they named Graciana as a master witch. Graciana's sister was assaulted with similar torture and finally confessed because she "was a woman of weak condition and little perseverance." The granddaughter confessed because her father threatened her with a dagger and a club. AHN, Inqu., Leg. 1679, images 1055, 1067.

this reason, there is very little improvement [in them], and then they
... do not say half of what they know.

In Elizondo, another unlucky death occurred in the past few days,
involving a most famous old witch who carried away children there.
They took all possible measures with her to get her to confess, and she
always was variable, confessing something one day and denying it all
the next. They were not able to get her to name a single accomplice.
In this state, the unfortunate woman died. Being present at her death,
a confessed girl-witch said she saw a goat chewing the dead woman's
jawbones.

I am also adding to this letter the little that has been done in
Legasa, where I have been warned that residents have imprisoned
certain women, among them the wife of Eneko de Elizamondi: having
put her into the stocks, parents then stoned her for having infected
their children, and she is very ill. Last night, the witches suffocated a
child in Erratzu, without leaving a healthy spot on her entire body. As
a result, there has been turmoil in the village, and the villagers have
thrown into prison three or four of the women whom the children
say carried them to the *akelarres*. The villages are stirred up. I do not
have a solution for this situation. . . .

With some members of this treacherous sect, I have seen something remarkable, which is that they relay their guilt in their spontaneous confessions with what looks like great straightforwardness
and truth. Then, when it comes to naming accomplices, they shut
down, to the point that they say they have never known anyone else
who attends the *akelarres*, because everyone there goes covered up,
in disguise. This is impossible, given that these confessants are over
fifty years of age and confess that they have attended the *akelarres* for
more than twenty years. I am treating some of these people's confessions as incomplete. I am hoping they will confess entirely, and I am
exhorting them to do so.

The parish priests have very great labor with the witches who are
very publicly known but who refuse to confess and are *negativas*.[49]
With audacity and shamelessness, these witches are demanding that

49. The adjective *negativa* here
implies a person who persistently
denies something, in this case, who
refuses to confess to witchcraft.

priests hear their confessions and administer the Eucharist to them on the feast days of the Virgin Mary, and other major Catholic holidays. This is causing an enormous scandal, given that these women have been publicly testified against as witches, and named as the ones carrying away the children to the *akelarres*. It is provoking great distress for the women who have confessed to witchcraft, to see that they are excluded from the sacraments while the *negativas* are admitted to them. This is going to provoke even more concern when Easter comes. I beg Your Lordship to find a solution for this.[50]

I feel that there are certain respectable people in this sect of witches who wish to remedy their state. If Your Lordship were to use your customary mercy, Your Lordship might do them the favor of allowing them to be reconciled to the Church in secret, after they have made their spontaneous confessions. The Devil puts no greater obstacle in the way of people seeking to . . . return to God than the shame of going in person to the holy tribunal of the Inquisition in Logroño. Their journey and the point of it is public; in no way can they make the journey without publicity. I beg Your Lordship to look into this, and to advise me if this favor could be done for the aforesaid people if they make their spontaneous confession before me, since I, being here, could reconcile them to the Church.[51] With this measure, I am certain that many would come to confess spontaneously in a very complete way; via this road, we would save many souls and have more testimonies against those obstinate ones who refuse to confess, who are numerous. At this very moment, as I am writing this letter, people in this village of Elizondo have become stirred up over seven children who say publicly that a certain woman takes them to the *akelarres*, and they have put her into prison. I have not interfered in this from seeing that those who are agitated have become a little quieter with the imprisonments, and greater problems have been avoided. . . . Such things are occurring in a similar way all over this region.[52] No one would believe what is happening unless he sees it with his own eyes. . . .

50. Villagers who confessed to witchcraft could not receive the Catholic sacraments until they were absolved by an inquisitor or a representative of Pamplona's bishop.

51. Araníbar did not receive the permission he requested.

52. Araníbar is not relaying the entire truth, which is that he encouraged such imprisonments across multiple villages.

May God give Your Lordship many years with the increase of all
the good that Your Lordship deserves, and that I, the chaplain and
servant of Your Lordship, desire.

Friar Leon de Araníbar

From Elizondo, January 29, 1611

**LETTER FROM INQUISITION COMMISSIONER LEON DE
ARANÍBAR TO THE LOGROÑO INQUISITION TRIBUNAL
ABOUT EVENTS IN ZUBIETA, FEBRUARY 25, 1611[53]**

... Residents of the village of Zubieta are now sending three prisoners
to the inquisition jails [in Logroño] with their beds and twelve ducats
apiece.[54] They are:

+ Pedro Unaya, called Xeru
+ Maria de Mateorena or Echeverría, wife of Pedro de Arizu
+ Marijuana de Maritokoa

All three are leaders in the wickedness of Zubieta's *akelarres*, and the
most obstinate, insolent, and destructive people of this profession [of
witch] that I have [ever] seen. The damage they have done and continue
to do every day in this place is so great that it has been amazing they
have not been cut with knives. Licentiate Irigoyen, the rector of the
place, and most of the residents have insisted that I give them a letter
for Your Lordship. Their incessant entreaties and the compassion I
have for the place have conquered me, and especially the respect I
have for that rector Irigoyen, who has discovered the entire wickedness
through his industry and attentiveness. Up to now, I have never seen
such zeal and care in anyone; he is not even pardoning his relatives,
but has made even more efforts with them so that they would confess.

I do see that sending these three prisoners [to you] without [your]
order is a great extravagance. What I regret the most is that we cannot
justify it or satisfy Your Lordship about it unless you were to see
with your own eyes what is happening in this place concerning these

53. AHN, Leg. 1679, images 1–3,   54. Beds in early modern Navarre
excerpted.   could be carried by hand. See
                                      chapter 4.

witches. The three [being sent] are very much testified against by all the confessants of the previous report, as well as the report I am sending now; and besides what the reports say, there is the public voice of the children of the place.[55] Zubieta cannot contain more than fifty houses, and yet there are 103 bewitched babies [*criaturas*] within the past five months, and these three prisoners have done the greatest damage.

Xeru has been variable, confessing and denying, and even when his own son, a confessant, said he was a witch to his face, nothing could be done with him. Maria de Mateorena has always been unyielding, like a flint, and every person of her house is a witch except for a young shepherd. Marijuana de Maritokoa has made her confession and says things merely to comply, being a treacherous and experienced witch. I beg Your Lordship with the greatest emphasis, please do not return these witches to Zubieta if possible, so that the village may have the consolation of being calm for a bit. If the witches return, I fear they will be burned alive, though that might not be a bad idea. Xeru and Marijuana are poor, but Mateorena has a very good house and property.[56] . . .

May our Lord protect Your Lordship for a thousand years with the increase that I, your chaplain and most insignificant employee, desire.[57]

Leon de Araníbar

---

55. Araníbar's comment about the "public voice of the children" encapsulates perfectly a key dynamic in this witch hunt.

56. When inquisition prisoners were poor, the inquisition tribunal had to pay for their upkeep. Poverty-stricken prisoners also had little for the inquisitors to confiscate if they were found guilty.

57. There is no evidence that Araníbar ever acted as a religious chaplain or priest for the Logroño inquisition tribunal, though he was the abbot of the monastery of Urdax.

CHAPTER 2

Father and Son

Child witches in Olague publicly named Miguel de Imbuluzqueta as a witch in late March 1611; Imbuluzqueta's own son, Pedroco, identified him as a witch as well. Imbuluzqueta remained quiet for a time after the initial accusations. But on May 6, 1611, he publicly confronted Graciana de Olagüe at her front door and accused her of having coerced his son into naming his parents as witches.[1] In the process of this public encounter, Miguel slandered Graciana by calling her a witch and a thief, and Graciana promptly filed charges of defamation against him in the royal secular court in Pamplona. A few weeks after his arrest and placement in the royal jails, Miguel filed a countersuit against Graciana. The surviving trial transcript contains witnesses for both sides. Eventually, however, Miguel ran out of money, and he could not afford to keep his case moving forward. Ultimately, he was sentenced to exile, which was a standard punishment for defamation. We do not know whether he died in prison or after he left Navarre, but another secular legal case refers to his wife as a widow in 1615. Before his death, he told the Royal Court that neighbors in Olague had burned down his house. So far as we know, his wife and children continued to live in the village.

SOME IMPORTANT CHARACTERS, IN ORDER OF APPEARANCE

Graciana de Olagüe, the widow who sued Miguel de Imbuluzqueta for defamation

1. The material in this chapter come from AGN, *Tribunales reales*, #330569. The town name "Olague" does not carry an accent mark, though the surname "Olagüe" does.

Miguel de Imbuluzqueta, an adult witch suspect whom Olague's
children identified as a witch

Gaspar de Eslava, Graciana de Olagüe's prosecution lawyer

María de Alzate, prosecution witness for Graciana

Pedroco de Imbuluzqueta, the eight-year-old son of Miguel de
Imbuluzqueta

Juan de Urricola, Miguel de Imbuluzqueta's defense lawyer

Pedro de Ortiz, Olague's parish priest

Don Pedro de Echaide, a nobleman whose estate lay outside the
village

Juan de Unciti, Olagüe's blacksmith and first cousin to the village
priest, Pedro de Ortiz, as well as to Graciana de Olagüe

Guillendo de Oyeregui, young son of Miguel de Oyeregui, the
village woodworker

Don Martín de Unciti, a deacon in the Catholic Church, son of
Juan de Unciti, stepbrother to Marimartín de Unciti, and
stepson to María de Alzate, who was the second wife of Juan
de Unciti

Marimartín de Unciti, age twelve or thirteen, daughter to Juan
de Unciti and María de Alzate and stepsister to Don Martín
de Unciti

Doña Juana de Echaide, age eight, child witch, daughter of Don
Pedro de Echaide

MAY 17, 1611. CRIMINAL COMPLAINT FOR SLANDER,
FILED BY GRACIANA DE OLAGÜE AGAINST MIGUEL DE
IMBULUZQUETA, AND GRACIANA'S FIRST WITNESSES
[FOLS. 1R–5V, SELECTIONS]

I, Gaspar de Eslava, lawyer for Graciana de Olagüe, who is a resident
of Olague and the widow of surgeon Juan de Aldáz, criminally accuse
Miguel de Imbuluzqueta, resident of the same place. As part of this
accusation, I intend to prove the following four points, which our
witnesses will address:

Speaking without boasting, my party is an honorable woman, of good reputation, honest and quiet, who has never engaged in any sort of indiscretion, nor does she have the reputation of a witch. On the contrary, the accused, Imbuluzqueta, has a wicked reputation, and it is said publicly that he is a witch. Various times, a son of his, age eight, has confirmed it, and so have many other children, from which has resulted his wicked reputation.[2]

Next, when Holy Thursday last occurred [on March 31, 1611], the village priest of Olague made sure that all the children slept inside the church, on account of the fear that more would be bewitched. Some of the children had said that older witches would take fifty of them to the *akelarre* that night. Because that night was very cold, the priest asked my party to make a fire in her house, so that many children could go there to warm up; my party's house is directly in front of the church.[3] The children went into my party's house along with other neighbors, who are honorable men and women. If my party did not have a good reputation, her neighbors and the priest would have hesitated to send children into her house.

Next, on Friday, May 6, without any preceding reason or cause, the accused [Miguel de Imbuluzqueta] said to my party that she had made his son say that his parents were witches with threats and persuasions, and that his parents had bewitched him.[4] And for this reason, [she] had taken his son into [her] house on the night of Holy Thursday. In fact, the defendant's statements are the reverse of what happened, because before and after Holy Thursday, his son and many other [children] voluntarily and publicly said that the defendant was one of the witches. My party never persuaded the defendant's son to say his father was a witch.

2. Public insults by children were just as harmful as ones uttered by adults. Being named a witch by one's own child was especially horrific because the community believed the child would have no reason to lie.

3. It was common in this witch hunt for adults to put children into churches, as protection.

4. Evidence from other court cases suggests that parents of child witches often spent some time investigating their statements to see if the children remained consistent. That practice could account for the gap between March 31, when Miguel's son was allegedly coerced into a false accusation, and May 6, the date of Miguel's public confrontation with Graciana.

Next, on the night referred to above, May 6, the accused publicly called my party a witch, whore, thief, and a [criminal] accessory, as well as other offensive words. And he wanted to kill her, and he unsheathed a knife with his right hand in order to do so, and he would have hurt her if others had not intervened. . . . The accused kept vowing and repeating the injurious words, and thus hoped to give my party a wicked reputation, as our witnesses will attest.[5]

THE ACCUSED WAS INFORMED OF THE CHARGE, MAY 17, 1611

I, the undersigned notary, tell Miguel de Imbuluzqueta—named in the written petition and accused in the complaint—that if he wishes to make a plea, he should present me with it, as the court is ready and fit to accept it. Having understood this statement, Miguel de Imbuluzqueta said he considers himself notified and therefore will carry out his own proceedings. He said this with witnesses being present, namely Don Pedro de Echaide and Juan de Ortiz, residents of this village.[6] . . .

THE COLLECTION OF PROSECUTION TESTIMONY BEGAN ON MAY 16, 1611

Prosecution witness María de Alzate, age thirty-nine[7]

. . . She has known Graciana de Olagüe, the complainant, since she has had the use of reason. . . . And at no time has it been said or understood that the complainant is imprudent,[8] nor does she have the reputation

5. Imbuluzqueta intensified his public insults by repeating them, and the alleged threat of physical violence underlined the seriousness of his attack. Given the culture of honor in Navarre, he had to have known that he was risking a lawsuit for defamation.
6. As the reader will see shortly, Don Pedro de Echaide was occasionally

present when Olague's children were encouraged to name themselves as witches.
7. This María de Alzate is not the same María de Alzate who was married to Olague's blacksmith, Juan de Unciti.
8. The noun used here is *liviandad*, which carries connotations of lust.

of being a witch or anything else [dishonorable]. On the contrary, the accused has an evil reputation, and it is said publicly in the village that Miguel de Imbuluzqueta is a witch. On May 6, in front of this witness, all the children of the village said to Miguel, to his face, that he was a witch, and they said publicly that they went every night to the *akelarre*, and they said, screaming, that he took them, along with his own wife and son. They said that when they dance, he always goes in front. . . . The children said all of this publicly to the accused, before this witness and many other residents of the village. As a result, this witness and the other observers remained very frightened. This is what this witness knows about the question.

. . . This witness says she knows that on May 6, the present month, the accused went to the door of Graciana's house, . . . and in front of this witness, he told Graciana that on the night that the children went to get warm in her house [March 31], she told his son, with threats and persuasions, to say that his parents were witches. The contrary was true, because this witness, as she has already said, was with the children in Graciana's house on that night of Holy Thursday for the entire time, but she never saw or understood that Graciana had spoken or said anything to the son of the accused. If she had said something, without doubt this witness would have heard it.

. . . To the fourth question, this witness says that on the same day [May 6], the defendant publicly accused the complainant, at her own door, of being a thieving witch, and he put his hand on a knife that he carried in his belt. It seemed to this witness that he would have hurt her if he had not been impeded by others who happened to be present, given how angry and worked up he was, and this is what she knows.

Prosecution witness María de Olagüe, wife of García de Ciaurriz

. . . She was with the plaintiff at her door. The accused [Miguel de Imbuluzqueta] came to the door and without any reason or cause, said to the plaintiff that on the night of Holy Thursday, when the children were in her house, she made his son say, through threats and persuasions, that his parents were witches. And the plaintiff responded, "Watch what you say. The entire village knows that [I] didn't speak a word to [your son] on that night, and no one persuaded [your] son to say that his father and mother took him to the *akelarre* and were witches." Imbuluzqueta responded that even if nothing happened [on March 31], the plaintiff [still] made [his son] say it.[9] . . . This witness was there in the plaintiff's house on the night in question [March 31], . . . and she never saw the plaintiff speak a word to the accused's child.

. . . Next, what she knows is that without any cause, [on May 6] the accused began to treat the plaintiff badly with words, saying that she was a thieving witch and a wicked woman. Then the accused put his hand on a dagger than he had in his belt, and he wanted to injure the plaintiff with it, . . . and he was agitated and angry. She knows that all the children who say they go to the *akelarre* have said publicly, screaming, that the accused and his wife were witches, and that he always danced in front [in the *akelarre*]. . . .

THE COLLECTION OF DEFENSE TESTIMONY BEGAN IN THE SECOND HALF OF MAY 1611

The first defense witness for Miguel de Imbuluzqueta was his son Pedroco, age eight [fols. 15r–22r, selections]

On May 19, 1611, in the village of Olague, the undersigned notary acts upon a plea given in the Royal Court of Navarre by Miguel de Imbuluzqueta, resident of Olague. . . . To obtain proof of what is contained in [Imbuluzqueta's] complaint, I received an oath in the necessary legal form from Pedroco de Imbuluzqueta, son of Miguel de Imbuluzqueta. . . . Pedroco said he is eight years old, more or less, and although he is the son of the defendant, he will only speak the truth.[10] Asked about the second question, what he knows and can say is that on the most recent Holy Thursday, he went from the church to the house of Graciana, the complainant, to get warm, along with many other children

9. The children's stories about being pressured on Holy Thursday in Graciana's house were not consistent as to date.

10. Legally, Pedroco should have been too young to swear an oath. Boys aged fourteen and over and girls twelve and over were judged sufficiently mature to swear to tell the truth.

of the village. While they were getting warm in her kitchen, Graciana said to this witness, in front of the other children, that his father and mother were indeed witches, and this witness replied that they were not.[11] Graciana responded that this witness had to say that his parents were witches, and that Olague had another five adult witches beyond his own parents, and he had to say so publicly. In order to achieve her goal, Graciana wheedled and induced this witness with food and drink to say so, and she made him say that his father and mother were witches . . . when the truth was the opposite.[12] He said so out of fear of abuse, and this is what he knows and this is the truth. Hearing his statement read back to him, he ratified but did not sign it because he did not know how to write.

Defense witness María Martingorrincoa, age eighty-eight

. . . She has known the countercomplainant for more than thirty years; he is an honorable person, fearful of God and of his conscience, of good standing and opinion and reputation.[13] . . . Twenty-two years ago, a little more or less, the complainant Graciana de Olagüe sent a servant to this witness's house. The servant said that her mistress had sent her to ask to borrow some tongs to break open a cabinet, because her mistress had misplaced the cabinet's keys. Believing the servant was telling the truth, this witness sent the tongs. And within an hour of sending the tongs, this witness had another visitor, the daughter-in-law of Juan de Alzate, who came to ask if this witness had given tongs to someone, because the daughter-in-law had found a cabinet or chest of her father-in-law broken open. This witness replied that she had given tongs to the servant of Graciana de Olagüe, because the servant told her she needed them to break into a cabinet of Graciana's own house, where they kept the cooking oil. The daughter-in-law

11. Pedroco's later testimony left out the Holy Thursday incident at Graciana's house.

12. Later in the trial, Pedroco and another boy, Guillendo de Oyeregui, would state that Graciana made them drunk.

13. The fact that some of Miguel's defense witnesses had known him for so long should have made their depositions especially forceful.

of Juan de Alzate went away, and within a short time, everyone was saying publicly in Olague that with the tongs this witness had lent her, Graciana de Olagüe had broken open a cabinet of Juan de Alzate and had taken some money.[14] This is public knowledge in the village, although the village learned later that the money was restored to Juan de Alzate and he was satisfied with that.[15]

Defense witness María Michetorena, widow of Miguel de Michetorena, age seventy

. . . She heard from other adults that Graciana de Olagüe coerced Miguel de Imbuluzqueta's son. In order to make him say such things, Graciana hung up the son on her hearth, and gave him food and drink. Even though this witness did not personally see it, it is well-known [notorio] in the village. . . .

Defense witness María de Etulain, wife of Domingo de Alzate, age fifty

. . . When Juan de Alzate's daughter-in-law saw that his house had been robbed, she began to scream to the neighbors that people had robbed the house. When this witness, along with others, arrived at the house, they found the cabinet broken open. . . . This witness and other neighbors then went to Graciana's house because she was the only one at home, everyone else being in the fields. Having called Graciana into a room and charged her with the theft, Graciana confessed that it was true that she had broken open the cabinet and taken a bag from it, with papers and some coins, and the Devil made her do such a despicable act, and she would return it all. This witness does not know and could not say how much money was in the bag, but afterward, it was said publicly that Graciana had returned all the money to Juan

---

14. If Graciana's theft could be attested, then Miguel would not have slandered her in calling her a thief.

15. Juan de Alzate was the father of María de Alzate, who was married to blacksmith Juan de Unciti.

de Alzate. Because Graciana and Juan were first cousins, Juan did not press charges, and this is the truth.

Defense witness María de Alzate, wife of Juan de Unciti[16]

... What she can say is that eight days after the last Holy Thursday, [on Friday, April 8], in front of this witness and other women in the public street of Olague, the son of Miguel de Imbuluzqueta said that Graciana de Olagüe had made him say that his father and mother were witches. When the boy had replied that he would not say such a thing, Graciana de Olagüe had tied him up and suspended him in the air from the kitchen hearth.[17] ... This witness heard that on Friday, May 6, Miguel and Graciana had a litigious [*contenciosa*] quarrel.... This witness says that twenty-two years ago, when she was in the village of Lantz, where she lived with her [first] husband at the time, one day in August, her father, Juan de Alzate, now dead, who then resided in Olague, came to visit her, because she had recently given birth.[18] As soon as her father came into her house, he began to complain, saying that Graciana de Olagüe had gotten into a cupboard and had taken a piece of money from him. Some women in Olague had found her with the sack. Her father came to her house extremely angry from the pure feeling of torment, but she does not know nor can she say how much money was taken, except that a few days later, she heard her father say that Graciana had returned part of it.[19]

16. María de Alzate, whose name here in the trial transcript was given as María Olague, was the daughter of the theft victim Juan de Alzate. Married for a second time to Juan de Unciti, Olague's blacksmith, she was the mother of Marimartín. See later in this chapter as well as chapter 4.

17. A common local method of torture in this witch persecution was to tie witch suspects into trees and leave them hanging there.

18. María de Alzate and Juan de Unciti each had children from their first marriage, but in María's case, the sources relay nothing about them.

19. Again, the defamation charge against Miguel de Imbuluzqueta in May 1611—for calling Graciana a thief, among other things—would have been weakened if the theft had actually occurred.

When the royal notary summarized the results from Imbuluzqueta's defense witnesses in May 1611, he noted that four individuals had stated that Graciana herself had called Miguel a dirty witch [brujo suicio] on May 6. Four more had affirmed that Graciana had been a thief in 1589, twenty-two years earlier.

Miguel de Imbuluzqueta was imprisoned in the royal jails in Pamplona by May 26, 1611. On May 28, he sent a petition to the Royal Court, asking to be released and asserting that his children were dying from hunger.

DEFENSE FOR MIGUEL DE IMBULUZQUETA

Statement from Miguel's defense attorney, June 3, 1611 [fol. 38r]

Juan de Urricola, legal representative for Miguel de Imbuluzqueta, says that his client was passing through the street on the day of the litigious quarrel, and Graciana treated him very insultingly, with very ugly, offensive, and prejudicial words, to the effect that he was a low, dirty, vile man and a witch. She thus gave him enough of a reason for vigilante justice. She has also offended him through her writings [*por sus escritos*], treating him as a witch.[20] She has placed him in this reputation, basing her remarks on the words of children, none of whom should be given any credit whatsoever. . . . Malicious people are saying and publicizing that other people [in the village] are also witches, and many honorable people of Olague are defamed. People have found these rumors and public statements to be false through experiments . . . as the witnesses will state in more detail.[21] Because of all this, Graciana deserves to be condemned with great and rigorous criminal penalties.

20. The phrase "through her writings" is unclear. It would have been most unusual for Graciana de Olagüe to have been literate. Miguel's attorney may be referring here to Graciana's legal efforts, which resulted in written documents. Legal proceedings in the Royal Court in Pamplona were not subject to any rule of secrecy.

21. By June 3, 1611, Urricola had learned about the experiment performed on the dead priest of Aritzu, who was supposed to have been eaten by witches. See later in this chapter.

On June 13, 1611, Imbuluzqueta's defense lawyer, Juan de Urricola, filed a petition to the effect that Miguel was still a prisoner in the royal jails, though on Saturday, May 28, the Royal Court had ordered that Miguel be given complete liberty. In return, Miguel had pledged to come to court and to pay bail; the bail for Miguel was coming from the judge-mayor [alcalde] of the village of Lantz. Both Miguel's release and the bail payment eventually occurred.

On June 13, 1611, Imbuluzqueta and his lawyer filed a formal counter-lawsuit against Graciana de Olagüe in the Royal Court, "over certain words and other matters," and asked that Miguel's witnesses be heard.

On July 1, 1611, the Royal Court agreed to collect information for Imbuluzqueta's case against Graciana.

Another statement by Juan de Urricola, Miguel Imbuluzqueta's lawyer, dated July 4, 1611 [fol. 51r]

First, babies [*criaturas*] of the village of Olague—certain ones in particular—have said and proclaimed that my client and his wife, and others, are witches. They have said this because of the great persuasion, bother, and vexation that has been inflicted on them by the parish priest of Olague [Pedro de Ortiz], Don Pedro de Echaide, and Juan de Unciti, the blacksmith. Other specific residents have also united on purpose to pressure the children into saying they were bewitched, and then calling other residents witches whom those adults have named. This persuasion has occurred because of the very evil hatred that these adults have for my clients and other residents, which is without foundation.[22] . . .

Without any force or violence, the young children have made known how they were persuaded [into witchcraft accusations] by

22. When Urricola stipulated that the hatred for his client was "without foundation," he meant it was without cause. The surviving evidence does not clarify why certain villagers in Olague were enemies of Miguel de Imbuluzqueta.

adults.[23] Specifically, Juan de Unciti, the blacksmith, persuaded a daughter of his to say that her mother was a witch, as well as other persons, on account of the hatred that he had toward his wife and others. His daughter has made known what her father did . . . and that it wasn't true that her mother was a witch. Juan de Unciti, her father, has treated his daughter very badly on account of what she has said. He has put her out of his house until she goes back to what she said before.[24] . . .

MORE DEFENSE WITNESSES FOR MIGUEL DE IMBULUZQUETA, JULY 4–10, 1611

Don Juan de Ettailaín y Garro, age thirty-five, parish priest of Ettailaín [fols. 84v–86r]

This witness has known Miguel de Imbuluzqueta for twenty years.[25] Two months ago, more or less, on a day that he cannot recall, he found himself in Olague with the village priests of Lantz and Aritzu. And it was imprinted on his memory that a son of Miguel de Imbuluzqueta, named Pedroco, age eight or nine, came before all of them and said he wanted to confess, freely, from his simple and spontaneous will, without being lured or called.

Asked what he wanted to confess, Pedroco responded that through the persuasion and inducements of Graciana, the plaintiff— who gave him so much to drink that his senses were disturbed—she made him say and make public that he and his parents, and the wife of Juan de Cheberría and his two daughters, and other honorable people of Olague were witches, against all truth. And that he had seen them in the gatherings of witches called *akelarres*, and this was not so, but

23. In other words, no one threatened or induced the child witches to say that they originally had been coerced into witchcraft confessions and accusations.

24. Marimartín talked at length, inside and outside court, about what she had suffered from her father and stepbrother; see later in this chapter and chapter 4.

25. Again, the duration of this witness's acquaintance with Miguel should have given his testimony extra weight.

false and a lie. In particular, when he [Pedroco] was called to the city of Pamplona by Dr. Muñariz, a commissioner of the Inquisition, he said the same, having been persuaded the whole way there by a son of Graciana de Olagüe, who threatened and menaced him, saying that he would have to kill him if he varied in any detail from what he was supposed to say.[26] That son took out a knife to frighten him. Due to those threats and persuasions, he had falsely sworn and said a lie, because he had never been taken to those diabolical gatherings, nor did he know what it was to be a witch, nor could he have truthfully named others, or anyone at all. He confessed and publicly declared the offense he had committed. He was impassioned.

An hour later, another boy came to them: this one was named Guillendo de Oyeregui, son of Miguel de Oyeregui, the woodworker, and Juana de Arrechea. Crying, Guillendo said that Juan de Unciti, the blacksmith, had caught him alone in the field called Larrica, and threatened him with a club, saying he would have to kill him if he did not say that Unciti's own wife, as well as a daughter of Domingo de Alzate, and the wife and daughters of Juan de Cheberría, and other people, whom other boys had pointed out, were witches.[27] Because of the state of terror in which Unciti put him, and the persuasions, he said in the field that he would say it publicly in the village. By doing so, he had committed a very great offense against those he had named, when it was not the truth, but a lie. . . . This witness and the other priests were amazed that this boy would have had the nerve to say something publicly that he did not really know, and which was not true. The excuse the boy gave was the vexations carried out by Juan de Unciti, and the fact that Unciti threatened to beat him to death with a club unless he said and made public the accusations of witchcraft.[28]

26. In other child witches' depositions, it was not Graciana's son who accompanied the youngsters to Pamplona but Juan de Unciti's son, Don Martín de Unciti.

27. Domingo de Alzate was María de Alzate's brother and hence Juan de Unciti's brother-in-law. There are no other references to Domingo's daughter as a witch.

28. Death by clubbing was not unusual in early modern Navarre. The question is whether an adult could have beaten a child to death in his own village and gotten away with it. Homicide was firmly gendered male in Navarrese culture.

This is what both boys confessed freely in front of the other village priests and this witness. Afterward, the boys have remained firm in their statements, without wavering in any detail.[29] This is what this witness has heard them confess and say. This witness makes his deposition with the solemn declaration that no spilling of blood or bodily mutilation shall arise or result from it.[30]

Defense witness Juan de Ascarraga, field worker, age forty-six [fols. 86r–88r]

... Recently, there has been a public clamor in Olague that the plaintiff, Graciana de Olagüe, and her son, and Martin de Unciti, a student, took into Graciana's house Pedroco de Imbuluzqueta, son of Miguel de Imbuluzqueta, as well as other young boys. [There] they forced the youngsters to say and publicize in Olague, in front of adults, that Pedroco and his parents, and the wife of Juan de Cheberría, and two of Cheberría's daughters ... and other honorable people were witches, and have been seen in the gatherings the witches hold. They suborned and gifted the children with food and drink, and sometimes threatened them with mistreatment. These acts have been revealed by the same children, who have said publicly that Graciana de Olagüe, in her own house, with her son, Sancho, and Martín de Unciti, brought them to say what they neither knew nor had seen, against all reason, intimidating them with mistreatment. . . .

Today, this witness remembers how the week before St. John's day [June 24], he came one day to the house of María de Alzate, the wife of Juan de Unciti, the blacksmith; she was one of the reputed witches. There, María de Alzate called in a daughter of hers, a girl of twelve or fourteen [named Marimartín]. In the presence of this witness, along

---

29. This priest, who lived in a different village, knew that Guillendo and Pedroco remained consistent in revoking their confessions. His knowledge speaks to communication networks.

30. Ettailaín y Garro's statement about "spilling of blood" was an attempt to prevent his testimony from provoking vigilante justice or additional legal proceedings. There was no principle of secrecy in the secular legal system. Onlookers would have known that Ettailaín y Garro had been called to testify, and he could have spoken freely about what he had said. He realized his testimony was explosive.

with Miguel de Arraíz, the miller, Miguel de Cheberría, and other adults, María de Alzate asked her daughter, with great gentleness, to say where, when, and how she had seen that her mother was a witch.[31] She told her not to hesitate to speak in front of the adults who were there.[32] Pouring tears, the girl answered that she did not know that her mother was a witch, nor had she seen as much, nor could she say so truthfully. Then María de Alzate returned to charging her daughter, and asked if she knew for certain that her mother was a witch, and if she did not know it, how and why had she publicly said that she was one.

At this, the daughter, who was not induced or frightened, said that her brothers [sic] had taken her to the house of Graciana de Olagüe, and Graciana's son Sancho was there, and another boy. . . . Graciana was helping, and they put it into the heads of every child they collected there that they should say and affirm they were witches, and that she and her mother were as well, along with five other people from the house of Juan de Cheberría. They told her to tell the truth and not deny it. Pressured by their statements and forcibly persuaded by their threats, she came to believe that what so many said must be true. With this trickery, they made her say and publicize that she and her mother, along with the wife and children of Juan de Cheberría, were all witches. In particular, Martín de Unciti, her brother, pressured her to be firm in what she had confessed, and not to deviate from what her companions said, or else he would have to throw her over the dam.[33] Thus, she said and publicized what they wanted, and it was not true, nor had she ever seen or known anything about witches.

Afterward, this witness has seen that this girl has been persistent in saying and confessing that people in Graciana's house persuaded her with foods, drinks, and threats into [saying] what she did not know or had ever seen.[34] . . . When [the girl's retraction] came to the notice

---

31. The encounter between the adolescent Marimartín, her mother, and the other adults is also reminiscent of a communal ceremony of confession and forgiveness, even if it occurred in a private home.

32. Miguel de Cheberría may have been related to Juan de Cheberría, whose wife and daughters had been accused of witchcraft.

33. As the reader will see, Don Martín de Unciti was actually the stepbrother of his much-younger sister, Marimartín.

34. Like Ettailaín y Garro, Ascarraga was also attentive to consistency over time in the child witches' revocations of their allegations.

of her father, Juan de Unciti, he threw her out of the house because she had not wanted to return to saying that her mother and the rest were witches. Furthermore, the girl said that at the time the persuasions and threats were going on in the house of Graciana de Olagüe, Graciana specifically, repeatedly said that Juan de Cheberría was rich and had money, and thus no one should debate or doubt saying that his wife and daughters were witches, and that they had been seen in the *akelarre*.[35] . . .

At this point, those in the house said good-bye to this witness, and this is what he knows and has heard.

Defense witness Miguel de Arraíz, a miller, age fifty-one [fols. 88r–90r]

. . . About a month ago, a little more or less, this witness found himself in the company of Miguel Seme, a resident of Olague, and the village priests of Lantz and Aritzu, and they were in good conversation. This witness recalls very well that two young boys came before the priests. One was the son of Miguel de Imbuluzqueta; the other was the son of Miguel de Oyeregui, the woodworker. Without any force or violence, bribes, gifts, or inducements, but moved only by their free will, the boys said that days earlier, they had been gathered in the house of Graciana de Olagüe, the widow, where a son of hers and Don Martín de Unciti gave them bread to eat and wine to drink, and made them believe that other children from Olague had confessed that they were witches, and said the two boys were as well. . . . And so the two boys had to say publicly that they were witches too.[36] As a result, they affirmed that Miguel de Imbuluzqueta was a witch, and they conformed to everything the other children said. . . .

---

35. The meaning of this sentence is uncertain. Was Graciana de Olagüe implying that the Cheberría family deserved witchcraft accusations because of their alleged wealth?

36. During this witch hunt, children who were named as witches could suffer popular, vigilante justice unless they got ahead of the story by either confessing to witchcraft or relaying that they had been taken to the Devil's *akelarre* by force. Homza, *Village Infernos*, 22–23.

Besides, this witness recalls that fifteen or twenty days ago, he found himself with Juan de Ascarraga and other people from Olague. Marimartín de Unciti, age twelve or fourteen, the daughter of Juan de Unciti, the blacksmith, came before them. In the presence of everyone, she said that she had been induced and threatened in the house of Graciana de Olagüe by Graciana, Graciana's son Sancho, and Don Martín de Unciti . . . to say publicly that she and her mother, María de Alzate, were witches. . . . Don Martín de Unciti, her brother, told her he would have to kill her if she did not say this. . . . And so, imposed upon in this way, she persisted in making public statements about witchcraft that were deceptions and lies, making everyone believe what was not true.

Then Marimartín said that when she was taken by Don Martín de Unciti with other children to the city of Pamplona, to appear before Dr. Muñariz, a commissioner of the Inquisition, all the way there Don Martín was persuading them with food and drink to be uniform in their statements, and not to deviate from what they had publicly said. With his persuasion, they said and deposed that they all had been taken to the *akelarre*, and that they were witches, and so was María de Alzate [Marimartín's mother], and the wife of Juan de Cheberría and his daughters, and other persons. . . .

The former village priest, now dead, was a very good priest, without a doubt: he led an excellent life and served as an excellent example. . . . Upon his death, the children raised a lie, namely that witches took his body from his tomb and ate it.[37] To know whether it was true or not, this witness remembers very well that Dr. Etxalar, a canon in the cathedral of Pamplona, along with some members of the Society of Jesus and some priests, came to Olague and carried out an experiment: they publicly opened the tomb where the dead priest was buried.[38] This witness saw with his own eyes, together with everyone else present, that the dead body was entirely there, without being

37. This was the same priest who healed María de Alzate's arm when her husband, Juan de Unciti, broke it with a fire shovel. See chapter 4.

38. Unfortunately, the sources do not describe how much time had passed between the priest's burial and his later exhumation. A canon of a cathedral was an ecclesiastic who had a benefice and a yearly income from that church.

destroyed or lacking any part: the dead priest's arms were crossed, his feet and legs were unfolded, his religious cap was on his head, and he looked just as he did the day he was buried. For greater certainty, some people touched him; this witness in particular caught him by a foot and a leg, and moved them in front of everyone. Afterward, people remained satisfied that the statements that the witches had carried away the body were false and contrary to the truth. And everyone concluded that what the children had said and were saying about the priest and the witches was a deceit and a lie.[39]

Pedroco de Imbuluzqueta ratified his original testimony for his accused father, Miguel, on July 6, 1611 [fols. 90v–91v]

... They read this witness his first deposition. He says he recognizes it. What he remembers is the same thing that he had said and declared in his first deposition. In order to make him say that his father and mother were witches, and that he himself was a witch too, Graciana de Olagüe and Don Martín de Unciti got him alone, and then deprived him of his natural reason by making him drink various times a great quantity of wine, undiluted with water. They made him drink by force and against his will. He was unable to leave because they tied his feet and hands with some cords or halters [for livestock], and hung him from the chimney, threatening to keep him there and maltreat him. Like a boy without capacity, transported out of his judgment by fears and threats, forced by them and their maltreatment, they made him promise that he would say outside the house what he had said inside of it.[40] They repeated many times that he and his father and mother, and the wife of Juan de Cheberría, and Cheberría's two daughters . . . were all witches, when this was false and completely against the truth.

He was like a child without the capacity or the natural reasoning to know and understand the offense and injury that he had done, having removed honor and good reputation from the people of Olague, and

---

39. Crucially, no one in Olague explicitly moved from lies about the dead priest being cannibalized to doubt that witches could exist.

40. Pedroco's account here does not mention Holy Thursday. It seems likely that he was taken or lured to Graciana's house on at least one other occasion.

hurting them with what he did not know and had not seen.[41] The cause of it all was Graciana de Olagüe and Don Martín de Unciti: the latter took this witness and other children from Olague to appear before Dr. Muñariz, a commissioner of the Inquisition, and they said what Don Martín and Graciana had persuaded them to say. He and the other children all testified in Pamplona without a single discrepancy, thanks to Don Martín's pressure.

Another boy, Guillendo de Oyeregui, testified for Miguel de Imbuluzqueta on July 6, 1611 [fols. 92v–93r]

Guillendo de Oyeregui, age eleven, son of Miguel de Oyeregui, the woodworker. . . . Graciana de Olagüe made this witness drink more than a pint of wine without water; with his judgment disturbed, she persuaded him to say that Miguel de Imbuluzqueta and his wife, the wife of Juan de Cheberría and his two daughters, and Pedroco de Imbuluzqueta, were witches. . . . They also took him to another house . . . where he saw Don Pedro de Echaide, Juan de Unciti, the blacksmith, and a student named Sancho. . . . And he [was told to] name many more persons as witches, including the daughter of the dead priest. He was persuaded most by Juan de Unciti and his son, Martín de Unciti. . . .

Defense witness Juana Mayor, age fifty [fol. 99v]

. . . About four months ago, the village was stirred up because of the children saying that they had been turned into witches. At the start of all this, this witness was walking along and found herself at the door of the house of Juan de Unciti, the blacksmith, . . . and she found there Don Martín de Unciti, and they began to talk about witches. Don Martín said that he would have to take his stepsister, Marimartín de Unciti, to Olague's dam, with ropes from the house.[42] And he would

41. Children's public insults were just as devastating as adults' with regard to honor.

42. This is the first moment in the surviving evidence when we realize

that Don Martín de Unciti and his much-younger sister, Marimartín, were stepsiblings.

have to make her reveal if she was a witch. This witness told him not to do it, because it was not good to make anyone say so through force, or with violence and mistreatment, but rather they should say so freely, from their own will. Don Martín replied that other children had confessed his stepsister was a witch, and in the end, he would have to make her confess through force. Afterward, this witness saw that Don Martín de Unciti took great care to tell the child witches that they should be firm and consistent in what they had declared, and he took them around with him, wherever he liked. He spoke to them constantly, and it seemed as if he wanted them to say much more than what they had already stated.

Defense witness María de Alzate, wife of Juan de Unciti, age fifty. María was the mother of Marimartín and the stepmother of Don Martín de Unciti [fols. 100v–101v]

. . . Regarding the dead priest, who died recently, his name was Don Garcia de Olagüe, and he was the parish priest of Aritzu. He was one of the most honorable priests and servants of God that ever existed in this life. He was most exemplary, and was known and reputed as such by all. A few days after he died, a rumor began to circulate that was completely false, namely, the children said that witches had eaten the dead priest's body. The priest's sisters and nieces were so upset by this rumor that they gave an order to open his tomb. This witness was there when it was opened, along with some residents of Olague and people from other villages. The parish priests of Olague, Lantz, Aritzu, Etulaín, and Egozkue were there as well. Dr. Etxalar, a canon of the cathedral of Pamplona, came to Olague for this same purpose, with two members of the Society of Jesus. Everyone saw with their eyes that the dead priest was there, with his legs and his feet in his shoes, just as complete as the day he was buried, without lacking anything. To settle the matter further, the body was moved and shaken, touched and felt. . . . And then they knew the rumors were false about witches eating the body.

. . . This witness confirms that Don Martín de Unciti is her stepson [*hijastro*]. With the evil motive and will that Don Martín has had and does have toward Miguel de Imbuluzqueta and his wife, he has gathered together children of Olague various times in his house, especially a son of Miguel de Imbuluzqueta and a daughter of this witness. He has been teaching [*industriando*] the children with compliments, gifts, offers, threats, and mistreatment, so that they might say and make public that they themselves are witches, along with their parents and other people. Graciana de Olagüe, in company with Graciana's son and Don Martín de Unciti, hoped and continues to hope to defame and insult many honorable and wellborn people of Olague, and to turn their lives upside down with sorrows and troubles. The parish priest of Olague [Pedro de Ortiz] has supported this business, though it lacks even a grain of truth. The priest has helped and defended what has been intended and stated by Graciana and her son, and this witness's stepson, Don Martín de Unciti. The parish priest of Olague has agreed with what these adults and the instructed, imposed-upon children have said, without paying attention to reason or truth. . . .

MORE PROSECUTION WITNESSES FOR GRACIANA DE
OLAGÜE TESTIFIED FROM JULY 13 TO 19, 1611

Prosecution witness Don Martín de Unciti, son of Juan de Unciti, stepson of María de Alzate, and stepbrother to Marimartín [fols. 64r–66v]

Presented as a witness, Don Martín de Unciti, deacon, native of Olague, twenty-three years old, more or less. He knows the litigants and is a relative of Graciana de Olagüe, in the fourth degree.[43] He has no personal interest in this case. . . . To the first question, he replied he has known Graciana de Olagüe since his childhood, from observation, interchange, and conversation. He knows she has been held, is held, and is reputed to be an honorable and honest woman who lives a retiring life, and as such he has held and does hold her. At no time has

---

43. In 1215, Pope Innocent III and the IV Lateran Council decreed that marriage was prohibited within four degrees of kinship: parent and child would be the first, siblings would be the second, uncle-niece or aunt-nephew would be the third, and first cousins would be the fourth.

he understood her to be frivolous or have the reputation of a witch. Such was said by Miguel de Imbuluzqueta, and since the Feast of the Resurrection, the children of Olague have said Miguel is a witch, and they have seen him walk in the *akelarres* with other witches when the dance there occurs. This has been confirmed and said many times by a child of Miguel's, who is eight years old, in conformity with what other children of Olague declare, without their being induced, forced, or threatened by anyone. . . .

To the second question, what he knows is . . . during the last Holy Week, children of Olague, of their own free will, began to declare that they were being taken to the gatherings of the witches, the *akelarres*. In particular, on Holy Thursday the older witches were promising to take fifty children from the Valle de Anue to the *akelarre*. With this news, the parish priest had reason to collect the children in the church to protect them from the witches, as he in fact did. By putting them in the church, he entrusted them to God. Once most of the night had passed, the priest made the children go across to the house of Graciana de Olagüe in order to get warm, because they were cold; this witness went along with them, accompanied by other honorable neighbors. Graciana's house is in front of the church and is the closest, and they were all there for a long time, getting warm. . . . The children were not mistreated, threatened, bribed, or induced to say anything by Graciana or by any other person, . . . and no one could truthfully say the opposite. . . .

To the fourth question, he said he knows nothing about it, because he was not present at the quarrel [between Graciana and Miguel]. . . .

To the second question, the witness added that the parish priest of Olague [Pedro de Ortiz], along with Don Pedro de Echaide (who owns the Echaide manor), Juan de Iriondo, and other persons of Olague had been heard to say that in the past, the son of Miguel de Imbuluzqueta said and confessed with conviction that his father took him to the gathering of the witches and had bewitched him. [Pedroco said this] in the presence of Licentiate Acosta, the royal prosecutor [for the Royal Court in Pamplona], as well as the parish priest of Lantz.[44] . . .

---

44. Testimony had to be ratified after it was given, or else it could not be used in legal proceedings. Here, Don Martín de Unciti is adding to his comments on the second query.

Prosecution witness Juan de Ortiz, the Younger [*el menor*], age twenty-eight [fols. 66v–68v]

... He knows the litigants, and as far as he knows, he is not related to any of them. ... He holds Graciana as an honorable woman, and in such reputation and opinion she has been and is held by everyone who knows her. She has never been understood to be anything else; she has no reputation for imprudence, nor does she have the reputation of a witch. ... In front of this witness, a son of Miguel de Imbuluzqueta, age eight, along with other children of Olague, have said and confessed that Imbuluzqueta is a witch, and as such they have seen him lead the witches' dance in the *akelarre*. The children have said so multiple times to Imbuluzqueta's face.

Adding to his comments on the second question, this witness also recalls that before this lawsuit began, the son of Miguel de Imbuluzqueta said and declared various times that his father was a witch who had bewitched him and taken him to the *akelarre*. The son said this in front of Licentiate Acosta, the royal prosecutor; Don Pedro de Echaide; the parish priest of Lantz; and others. This witness was present. Other children of Olague asserted the same thing, saying that they usually saw Imbuluzqueta lead the witches' dance in the *akelarre*. ...

One day, this witness was in the house of Juan de Iriondo, a resident of Olague, along with Don Pedro de Echaide, who owns the Echaide manor, and other residents, and Miguel de Imbuluzqueta, the accused, came to the house. Imbuluzqueta began to say that Graciana de Olagüe had made his son say that his father was a witch, persuading him to do so with threats and mistreatment, and hanging him from the chimney on the night of Holy Thursday. This witness then stepped up, as someone who knew the opposite, and replied in Graciana's defense that Imbuluzqueta had no reason to say those words, because Graciana was not the sort of woman to do such things, nor could anyone truthfully say that she had persuaded Imbuluzqueta's son or had said a word to him. Imbuluzqueta replied that his son had asserted as much to him. This witness replied that Imbuluzqueta's son had not told him the truth and he was deceived in believing him, and Imbuluzqueta should not provoke a quarrel among honorable people. Then a son of Graciana stepped up to defend his mother because of what Imbuluzqueta had said. To avoid vigilante justice [*via de hecho*],

Don Pedro de Echaide and Juan de Iriondo stopped Graciana's son and saw Imbuluzqueta off. Everyone there condemned Imbuluzqueta for his bad behavior and conduct.

Prosecution witness Pedro de Ortiz, Olague's village priest [fols. 70r–71v][45]

Don Pedro de Ortiz, age sixty-nine. He is a relative of Graciana de Olagüe in the fourth degree of blood relationship, but he will say nothing but the truth.[46] . . . Many adults were with the children in Graciana de Olagüe's house on the night of Holy Thursday. This witness understands clearly that Graciana did not speak a word to the son of Miguel de Imbuluzqueta, nor did she ask him anything, or threaten him. Nevertheless, this witness has heard that on different occasions and in different places, Miguel de Imbuluzqueta has charged Graciana with having pressured his son to say that his father was a witch and that his father took him to the *akelarre*. And that Graciana had hung the son from the hearth. This witness then had occasion to censure Miguel and to reprimand him, as he in fact did multiple times, for the testimony he was raising against Graciana. This witness charged Miguel a great deal to tone down what he was saying, reminding him of Graciana's goodness, because no one was going to believe such a thing, and he should not raise matters that could dishonor her. . . . He reminded Miguel of what had previously been heard from his own son and many other children, who declared him a witch, and who said they had seen him in the gatherings of the witches. This witness begged Miguel to confess the truth and save his soul. Nevertheless, being obstinate, Miguel persevered in saying to various persons that what his son said [only] occurred through the inducement and maltreatment that Graciana had carried out, which caused his son to lie.[47]

---

45. Ortiz could sign his name at the end of his deposition.

46. Thus, Pedro de Ortiz, Juan de Unciti, and Graciana de Olagüe were all first cousins.

47. Miguel's persistence in his public claims about Graciana speaks to the wider culture of honor in these Navarrese villages: he was determined to recapture his dignity, even if it put him in legal peril.

... Before this lawsuit was raised, he had heard that one afternoon, Don Pedro de Echaide, Juan de Iriondo, Juan de Ortiz, and other persons—and in particular, he heard it from Pedro de Aldaz—were with Miguel de Imbuluzqueta in Juan de Iriondo's house. Pedro de Aldaz charged Miguel with an evil act for having said that his mother [Graciana de Olagüe] had mistreated Miguel's son and had persuaded the son to say that his father was a witch.[48] Pedro de Aldaz asked Miguel to tone it down and not to put a mark against his mother, because she was not a woman of such dealings. Miguel contradicted Pedro, and offended him with insulting words, so that they came to argue, and if the men named above had not been present, a scandal [escándalo] would have ensued.[49]

Prosecution witness Doña Juana de Echaide, age eight
[fols. 74v–75v]

... Legitimate daughter of Don Pedro de Echaide and Doña Graciana de Ursua, his wife. No oath was received from her because she is so young. . . . This witness says she is eight years old, and she knows the litigants by sight, and she does not know if she has any kinship with them. She has not received gifts, nor has she been induced or terrorized [regarding her statements]. For several months, she has been taken to the gatherings of the witches with a little brother of hers: three times, she has been taken from the manor of the Echaide. The people who have taken her are a woman from Olague named [Margarita], who also has taken Sancho, a son of Graciana de Olagüe.[50] The first time Margarita took her, she presented her to a goat that was in the witches' gathering, and said she had brought Juana for his service. Afterward, they danced with all the other witches who were in the akelarre. Among those witches, she recognized for certain Miguel de Imbuluzqueta, with his wife and children, one of whom was her

48. This is the first mention of Graciana having another son besides Sancho.
49. "Scandal" signified social disorder and tumult.

50. Margarita de Olagüe and her daughter, María Martín de Olagüe, were accused of witchcraft and attacked in their homes by Don Pedro de Echaide and his wife. See chapter 3.

age. The three times she has been taken, they have made her dance by taking the hand of Miguel de Imbuluzqueta and the hand of Margarita, who took her there.

The reason she has not been taken more than three times is because she told her parents what was happening, and they have had her under continual watch, trying to keep her from sleeping every night, along with her little brother, and thus the witches have not taken them, nor could they, although Margarita has tried.[51] This witness has made the same public statements as the other children of Olague, and particularly the son of Miguel de Imbuluzqueta, who said publicly that he, his mother, and many other adults of Olague were and are witches, and have been seen dancing in the *akelarre*, and committing serious sins.

Prosecution witness Juanico de Olagüe, age eleven [fols. 75v–76v]

... He does not know if he has any kinship with the litigants, nor has he received gifts or been terrorized, induced, or suborned [regarding his statements]. . . . He was in Graciana de Olagüe's house with the other children, getting warm at her hearth, where they spent part of that night. As an eyewitness, he knows for certain that Graciana did not speak a word to the son of Miguel de Imbuluzqueta, nor did she persuade him with food and drink, nor did she maltreat him with actions or words so that he would say something against his father. . . . Rather, that night this witness saw that the boy said freely, without any pressure from anyone, that Miguel, his father . . . with his mother, took him to the witches' gatherings. This witness knows this fact is true, because this witness is one of the child witches of Olague; he was bewitched by his godmother. In the *akelarres*, he has seen them dance and speak with the Goat. . . . This witness has seen many other child witches from the village in the *akelarres*. And all of them, with one voice, publicly and repeatedly told Miguel de Imbuluzqueta to

51. Throughout this witch hunt, Navarrese parents kept their children awake at night or tied them to their beds to prevent witches from snatching them.

his face that he was a witch. Miguel's wicked reputation has resulted from their statements, not because Graciana stirred anything up, nor does she have any blame in the matter, and this is the truth, even without the oath.

Prosecution witness Miguel de Olagüe, age fifteen [fol. 77r]

. . . Son of Miguel de Olagüe, took an oath according to law. He has been and is one of the child witches of the village, and he is among those who have gone for a year to the witches' *akelarres*. Along with many other children who also have been bewitched, this witness has confessed to being a witch before Olague's priest. He remembers very well that the priest collected them in church on the night of Holy Thursday to defend them from the older witches, who had promised to take fifty children before the Goat. Having passed much of the night in the church in the cold, the priest made them go to Graciana's house, so that they could get warm, and this witness found himself there with Miguel de Imbuluzqueta's son. That son was eight years old. He saw with his own eyes that Graciana did not speak a word to that boy, or give him anything to eat or drink, or persuade him, or mistreat him by action or word so that he would say anything against his father, or anyone else. Nor did she tie his feet or hands, nor did she hang him up. Whoever says so is engaging in false testimony.

. . . That same night, that boy [Pedroco] said in front of everyone that he was a witch, and his parents took him to the witches' gatherings. This witness knows that is true because he too has been taken by a brother-in-law of his, and he has seen Miguel de Imbuluzqueta with his wife and three children in those gatherings, dancing and occupying himself in vile and low tasks, and committing great offenses against God, Our Lord. Many other bewitched children of the village have seen the same thing when they were in the gatherings; all, with one voice, publicly and repeatedly, have told Miguel to his face that he is a witch. He has a wicked reputation from their having said and publicized it, not because Graciana did anything, nor has she stirred anything up, and she has no blame at all in the matter.

Prosecution witness Marichiparito de Lizaso, age eight [fols. 78r–79r]

. . . Legitimate daughter of Pedro de Lizaso, not taking an oath [on account of her age]. She was gathered in the church of Olague with many children of other residents, on order of the village priest, to defend them, so that the witches would not take them to their gatherings. At the end of a very long time, they went to get warm in Graciana's house, which is in front of the church. It is the closest house. The son of Miguel de Imbuluzqueta was there with all the rest. Graciana did not persuade him to speak against his father, or give him something to drink or eat, or threaten him, or carry out any maltreatment against him. This witness is very certain and assured about it, because she was an eyewitness.[52]

. . . This witness further states that she is one of the child witches of Olague, and as such, she has been taken by two women to the witches' gatherings, and she has seen there, among other persons, Miguel de Imbuluzqueta and his wife and two children. Typically, Miguel spends his time there dancing with the other witches, and occupying himself in vile and low tasks, offering himself to the Goat as his own, and saying he would not leave the Devil's flock even if they burned him, promising so much to the Devil that even his own breath would be his.[53] And then Miguel stops talking to the Devil and adores him in his filthy parts. . . . All this has been seen and is known by many other child witches of the village.

Prosecution witness Maraico de Sorauren, age twelve [fol. 79v]

. . . She took an oath. Last Palm Sunday, she was bewitched and taken for the first time to the gathering of witches. Since then, she has been

---

52. The fact that children understood the importance of eyewitnessing is noteworthy. All the evidence suggests that illiterate, Basque-speaking, Navarrese villagers knew how to use the courts.

53. The child witches' comments about burning reflect their awareness of the Inquisition's *auto de fe* in 1610.

taken many different times by a woman from the village, except on Holy Thursday, when she was kept awake with vigilance in the parish church of the village, along with many other bewitched boys and girls. Then she was in the house of Graciana to get warm, and she also remembers that the son of Miguel de Imbuluzqueta was there, too. . . . She knows for certain, as an eyewitness, that Graciana did not speak with Imbuluzqueta's son, or give him anything to eat or drink that night, or mistreat him, or tie him up or hang him from any part of his body, so that he would say something against his father.

. . . Since that Palm Sunday, she has seen Miguel de Imbuluzqueta and his son, with another younger child and Miguel's wife, in the witches' gatherings. And finally last night, late, Miguel was dancing, like he has done other times, and there he makes his promises to the Goat, to always be his servant, and not to betray him or leave his flock even if they burned him. Once he says that, he adores the Goat in his filthy parts. . . . And afterward, Miguel charges the children to keep secret what has gone on there, and he threatens them with fire if they do the opposite.[54] All this happened last night, and she saw many other older and younger witches who were at the gathering.

In September 1611, Miguel de Imbuluzqueta, who was out on bail, and his guarantor, Martín de Echeverría, fled into the neighboring province of Gipuzkoa.[55] When Echeverría returned to Olague in early October, he was given fifteen days to find Miguel and return him to prison. When he failed to do so, he was jailed until December 10, 1611, when Miguel must have returned or been found. The Royal Court referred to Miguel as a prisoner in February 1612.

54. Again, fire imagery was everywhere in this witch hunt. One form of local torture was to march suspected witches in ladders and swing lighted torches over their heads. Homza, *Village Infernos*, 46.

55. Echeverría was called a *fiador* in the trial, which signified a bondsman who pledged his own presence if the indicted person failed to show up.

PETITIONS FROM JAIL AND THE VERDICT

Petitions

February 21, 1612 [fol. 148r]: Miguel Imbuluzqueta was once more a prisoner.

March 2, 1612 [fol. 150r]: Miguel told the Royal Court that he was ill and asked to be released so that he could be cured. Though the surgeon of the jail had been called, the surgeon did not want to undertake a cure for him.[56]

March 25, 1612 [fol. 151r]: Miguel was ill in bed.

No date, 1612 [fol. 152r]: Miguel said that counselors for the Royal Court have seen his lawsuit against Graciana de Olagüe, [but] his lawyer was not present when it was read. He asked the royal viceroy to order the court reporter to read the case so that his lawyer might hear it, and he requested justice.

Miguel was still ill in prison on April 9, 1612.

The folios of this legal case are not foliated after April 9, 1612.

No date, 1612: Miguel de Imbuluzqueta, prisoner in the royal jails, said that regarding his case against Graciana de Olagüe, the court reporter does not wish to receive it, saying that Miguel cannot pay the fees. The supplicant [Miguel] is so poor that he has no way to pay the fees. Being ill, he suffers extremely for lack of provisions.[57] Given these circumstances, he begs the royal viceroy to order something provided for him, and to determine the case.

The verdict against Miguel de Imbuluzqueta, before April 14, 1612

The Royal Court finds him guilty of having said the injurious words contained in the prosecutor's accusation. . . . We condemn the accused to appear before a notary and witnesses, and publicly retract those words. We further condemn him to four years of exile from this kingdom [of Navarre], and he shall leave within six days to complete that sentence.[58]

---

56. We do not know whether the surgeon was declining treatment because Miguel could not pay him or because the surgeon believed treatment was not necessary.

57. As was the case with María Martín de Olagüe in chapter 3, Miguel desperately needed the charity of the jail's warden while he was imprisoned.

58. On the basis of my research, the Royal Court must have been persuaded

Miguel's reply to the verdict, April 14, 1612

. . . He is blameless in what he is accused of doing. He is of the same social status as Graciana de Olagüe, and he has been condemned because his great poverty would not allow him to pay for [more] collection of proof.[59] And he has to retract the words he has been accused of saying before a scribe and witnesses, and pay costs. Beyond all this, he is very sick in bed, in great danger of his life. May Your Majesty [the viceroy] order him freed on account of the bail he has posted. The bail, as well as the depositions of his character witnesses, are held by the mayor of Lantz. May Your Majesty note that from being so worn out with the costs of prison, he has nowhere else to turn.

We do not know whether Miguel de Imbuluzqueta died in prison or managed to leave for exile. In April 1612, while still in Pamplona's royal jails, he told the court that his house in Olague had been burned down by his neighbors.[60] Another Royal Court document involving Miguel's wife describes her as a widow in 1615.

to some degree as to Miguel's complaint, even though he could not finish his case due to poverty. Four years of exile was a relatively light penalty for defamation.

59. Social honor was not necessarily linked to money in early modern Navarre, or Spain, either.

60. House burning was a catastrophe in early modern Navarre, as there was no communal or charitable obligation to rebuild.

CHAPTER 3

The Echaide Family and the Two Widows

Six weeks after the witchcraft incident in chapter 2, another public episode ensued over suspected witches.[1] This one involved assault as well as defamation. Over the weekend of June 18 and 19, 1611, a noble couple—Don Pedro de Echaide and his wife, Doña Graciana de Ursua—left their manor to confront a young widow in Olague whom their children had named as a witch. On Saturday, Don Pedro beat that widow, María Martín de Olagüe, in her home. On Sunday, he returned with his wife to confront María Martín's mother, Margarita de Olagüe, in her home: there, Don Pedro assaulted the mother, Margarita, as well as another one of her daughters, Graciana. María Martín had fled to her mother's house after the Saturday attack; when Don Echaide appeared again on Sunday, she either jumped out a window or fled out the back of the house and fell into a creek. Witness accounts differed.

During the Sunday assault, Margarita's son, Miguel, entered the room with a dagger to fend off Don Pedro. As the Echaide couple left Margarita's house, Margarita and Graciana leaned out a window and screamed insults at them. Don Pedro instantly launched a case in the secular court over Miguel's aggression with the dagger, but from there, the prosecution went in multiple directions. Charges against Miguel seem to have not been followed up, presumably because he had been confronting an intruder in his mother's home.[2] The Echaide couple also complained that Olague's constable, Juan de Zozaya, had failed in his duty to arrest María Martín; moreover, they claimed they had been the victims of Margarita's slander. Finally, it appears as if Don

1. The material in this chapter comes from AGN, *Tribunales reales*, #41366.

2. María Martín, her sister Graciana, and their brother Miguel fled Olague in the aftermath of the Echaide attacks. Miguel and María Martín were found and imprisoned; we do not know what happened to Graciana.

Pedro asked the Royal Court to imprison María Martín as a suspected witch and the court complied, though its officers knew well the
Spanish Inquisition was formally in charge of the ongoing witchcraft
investigations.

Margarita and her children filed a countersuit from prison for
injuries committed by the Echaide couple. Unfortunately, they were
poor, which inhibited the progress of their case.[3] María Martín died in
the royal jails in Pamplona in early January 1612, after being imprisoned
for five months. Her mother, Margarita, was released from jail on bail
and was condemned at first to two years of exile.

The surviving legal dossier reveals villagers' fury over both María
Martín's death in prison and her mother's original sentence. Communities often were highly divided over witchcraft suspicions and
accusations. At the first stage of the trial, before María Martín died in
jail, her defense witnesses testified in vague terms. After she perished,
however, a number of her neighbors were fiercely critical of Don Pedro
and his wife and adamant about María Martín's and her mother Margarita's innocence.[4] The new depositions may have had an effect on the
Royal Court. In June 1612, that court endorsed the original sentence
of exile but, a month later, ruled instead that Margarita would not
have to leave Olague until her countersuit against the Echaide couple
was resolved. The surviving legal manuscript ends there. We do not
know if Margarita's countersuit was concluded or whether she was
eventually forced to leave her village.

It is important to note that the Echaide couple's attacks on María
Martín and Margarita occurred more than six weeks *after* the incident
between Graciana de Olagüe and Miguel de Imbuluzqueta in chapter 2.
Yet much of the initial trial testimony in the Echaide case occurred
before the depositions in the Imbuluzqueta case, which may have been

3. In September 1611, María
Martín's lawyer told the Royal Court
that she could not pay for taking
witness depositions because of her
extreme poverty. AGN, *Tribunales
reales*, #41366, fol. 122r.
    4. Upon María Martín's death, her
neighbors may have come together to

fund the taking of additional testimony.
In the village of Erratzu, for example,
parishioners pooled their money to
launch a legal case against their priest,
who had tortured them as suspected
witches: Homza, *Village Infernos*,
144–46; ADP, C/242-N, fols. 211v, 218v.

due to the Echaide family's noble status and their possible "pull" with the Royal Court in Pamplona.

SOME IMPORTANT CHARACTERS, IN ORDER OF APPEARANCE

Pedro de Echaide, age six, son of Don Pedro de Echaide and his wife, Doña Graciana de Ursua

Don Pedro de Echaide, a nobleman and the plaintiff, married to Doña Graciana de Ursua

Juana de Echaide, age eight, daughter of Don Pedro de Echaide and his wife, Doña Graciana de Ursua

María Martín de Olagüe, a widow and alleged witch, daughter of Margarita de Olagüe and sister to Graciana de Olagüe and Miguel de Olagüe

Doña Graciana de Ursua, wife of Don Pedro de Echaide and mother of Pedro and Juana de Echaide

Juan de Zozaya, the constable (*jurado*) of Olague

Margarita de Olagüe, widow and alleged witch, mother to María Martín de Olagüe, Graciana de Olagüe, and Miguel de Olagüe

Graciana de Olagüe, sister to María Martín de Olagüe and Miguel de Olagüe and daughter of Margarita de Olagüe, widow and alleged witch

Miguel de Olagüe, brother to María Martín de Olagüe and Graciana de Olagüe and son of Margarita de Olagüe, widow and alleged witch

Gaspar de Eslava, lawyer for Juan de Zozaya, Olague's constable

Juan de Urricola, lawyer for Margarita de Olagüe and María Martín de Olagüe, widows and alleged witches

WITNESSES FOR THE PLAINTIFFS

Prosecution witness Pedro de Echaide, age six, June 23, 1611
[fol. 5r]

The court receives as a witness the minor son of plaintiff Don Pedro de Echaide, who is six, as he states and as it clearly appears from the baptismal book that we have seen.[5] He was taken on June 15 of the present month, on a Wednesday, and on the following two days by a woman [text missing] named Grisallu [text missing], while being covered up with her skirts. . . .

Prosecution witness Juana de Echaide, age eight, June 23, 1611
[fol. 6r–v]

The court receives as a witness the minor daughter of plaintiff Don Pedro de Echaide, who is eight, as it clearly appears from the baptismal book. . . . She was taken to the *akelarre* that same Wednesday [June 15], as well as the next two nights, by María Martín de Olagüe, widow of Pedro de Zozaya.[6] She could not verify which meadows she was carried to, except that they looked like the ones around Olague. Before they went to the fields, they walked to a house that they call the notary's, and from it they carried away a boy named Sancho and his mother, named María de Olagüe. Beforehand, María Martín de Olagüe, the widow, hit this witness with some thorns and bit her while she was asleep; she was asleep because of the herbs with which María Martín had touched her, so that she would not awaken. María Martín touched her [with the herbs] on her chest, cheeks, and face.

At the Devil's *akelarre*, she saw a black figure in the shape of a goat, who said to María Martín de Olagüe that she was very welcome, and that this witness was pretty. And without another word, the witches began to dance, and this witness did so, too. . . . María Martín de

5. The Royal Court was concerned to verify Pedro's and Juana's ages and turned to baptismal records to do so.

6. This was the accused witch whom Don Pedro de Echaide first attacked in Olague.

Olagüe gave the children mouthfuls of food, with very black bread and very black meat, and they had to drink from a black cup. . . . To eat and drink, the witches opened the children's mouths with their fingers, and in this way, they made them eat and drink.[7] Then, when the witches stopped dancing, the Goat had sex with the women who were of age. María Martín de Olagüe told this witness that if she ever told anyone that she was the one who carried her away, this witness, her parents, and their manor of Echaide would be turned into dust.

Prosecution witness Miguel de Egozcue, age fifteen, June 23, 1611 [fols. 6v–7r]

. . . A brother-in-law of his named Miguel de Olagüe resident of the same village, has taken and continues to take him to the *akelarres* of the witches. He has done so for the past year or so. The *akelarres* take place in the meadows that are close to the village and the house of the village's confraternity. They all dance there. There is a black goat there. After the dance is over, they go home. This witness has seen Margarita de Olagüe and [her daughter] María Martín de Olagüe there, as well as the son and daughter of the Echaide family.

Male prosecution witness Eneko de Ilurdoz, age fifty-five, June 24, 1611 [fols. 11r–12r]

. . . It was heard and said publicly in Olague that Wednesday, June 15, as well as the following two nights, María Martín de Olagüe carried Don Pedro and Doña Juana de Echaide, children of the plaintiff and residents of the Echaide house and manor, to the witches' gathering. . . . And on June 19, in the morning, around 8:00 a.m., Doña Graciana de Ursua, the wife of the plaintiff, came to Olague, accompanied by two male servants, one female servant, and the two children. Doña

---

7. Modern historians argue that witchcraft in early modern Europe turned on a reversal of Christian and communal values and norms. Here, the children's description of what they ate reversed or inverted the qualities of desirable food.

Graciana was in search of Juan de Zozaya, the village's constable: she wanted him to go with her to the house called Mariquirena, in order to verify the truth as to who was taking her children to the *akelarre*.[8] . . .

Male prosecution witness and servant of Doña Graciana de Ursua, Miguel de Egozcue, June 24, 1611 [fol. 18r]

. . . He is named Miguel, and he is twenty-three years old. María Martín de Olagüe, the accused, who is the widow of Pedro de Zozaya, has taken the Echaide children two or three times to the Devil's gatherings. . . . This witness has understood from other children in Olague that they have seen María Martín de Olagüe many times in the *akelarres*. . . . Doña Graciana ordered him and another female servant to go into Olague with her, and coming into the street, they found there Juan de Zozaya, the constable, . . . and Doña Graciana told Zozaya to follow her until they reached a certain house, and told him that he had to seize a certain woman there. Zozaya replied that he could not seize anyone without a court order, but Doña Graciana took him by the hand and led him to the front door of the house called Mariquirena. Doña Graciana went into the house with this witness, and they thought the constable Zozaya was following them. This witness says that Doña Graciana wanted to go into a particular door, and before she could get there, Margarita and María Martín had closed it, and did not want to open it. This servant forced it open. And then Doña Graciana said to the two widows, "Where is that honorable woman who has been taking my children to the *akelarre*?" The widows replied that they did not take them. Then Doña Graciana's husband, Don Pedro de Echaide, arrived. . . .

---

8. Basque houses often carried names. The term for constable here is *jurado*: *jurados* were elected annually from the village's male residents. Their job was to maintain social peace. The mayors (*alcaldes*) of Navarrese villages were judges of first instance, which meant that they heard initial legal complaints from citizens: if they could not resolve the cases, litigation could move to the Royal Court in Pamplona.

There are discrepancies in the witnesses' accounts of what happened when in the house of Mariquirena. Witnesses disagreed as to whether both Don Pedro de Echaide and his wife, Doña Graciana de Ursua, arrived at the same time. They also differed as to who was in the room that the Echaide couple entered: the elderly widow Margarita and her daughter, the widow María Martín, or Margarita and another daughter, Graciana. Witnesses for both sides confirmed that Margarita's son, Miguel de Olagüe, came into the room while the Echaides were there and pulled a dagger. But deponents again disagreed as to who was injured: some reported that Miguel intended to attack Don Pedro; others said that Miguel had cut a finger of one of the Echaide servants; still others said that Doña Graciana had either a finger or a glove cut by the dagger. The letting of blood exacerbated the severity of any crime in early modern Spain. Numerous men were standing at the front door of Mariquirena when the Echaides entered, where they could hear but not see the confrontation.

Male prosecution witness, Juan de Iriondo, June 24, 1611 [fol. 14v]

. . . As Don Pedro de Echaide and Doña Graciana were leaving Mariquirena, the widow Margarita and her daughter Graciana said [from their window] that Doña Graciana was a wicked, evil woman, and that Don Pedro was a witch, a traitor, and an evil man with a bad face, and he did not have the face of a man, nor was he fit to deal with them, . . . and he was a damned false traitor, and those who dealt with him were heartless and treasonous, . . . and Don Pedro and Doña Graciana were making their children say false things by giving them food and drink. And they were as clean as he was, and even cleaner than he would be in his entire life.

Male prosecution witness, Juan de Munuzue, late June 1611 [fols. 16r–17v]

The plaintiff [Don Pedro de Echaide], this witness, and others are living in fear of their children being taken [by the witches], and the village is highly scandalized. Doña Graciana de Ursua told this witness to come with her, and this witness saw Doña Graciana tell Juan de Zozaya, the accused constable, to go with her to a certain house because Zozaya had to arrest a certain woman and take her to the inquisitor [Alonso de Salazar Frías, who was on visitation in 1611]. This witness and Doña Graciana's servants went into the house while Zozaya stayed at the door; Zozaya did not want to follow her even though she had told him to do so. . . . Miguel de Olagüe, the brother of the accused [María Martín, Margarita's daughter], went upstairs with a dagger and wanted to stab Don Pedro [de Echaide] in the back. Seeing this, this witness left his place and went to Miguel de Olagüe, and he put his arm on Miguel's and parried the blow. . . . The constable Zozaya then appeared and took away the dagger. With all this, things quieted down, and everyone left the room, leaving there Miguel de Olagüe, Margarita de Olagüe, and Graciana de Olagüe, the accused.[9] . . . And the accused told Doña Graciana de Ursua that . . . she herself took her children [to the *akelarre*].

Don Pedro de Echaide and his wife presented more than twenty pros-ecution witnesses. The summary of those depositions is not dated, but it was drawn up by early July 1611. The synopsis laid out the Echaides' case in sequential order. First, their own children, as well as others in the village, had named the younger widow María Martín de Olagüe as a witch who had taken them multiple times to the akelarre. Next, Echaide's wife, Doña Graciana, had traveled into Olague with servants and a daughter in order to confront María Martín de Olagüe over bewitching her children. Doña Graciana had expected help with this confrontation from Olague's constable, Juan de Zozaya; she and her husband claimed Zozaya had been ineffective. Finally, after the Echaide couple physically confronted María Martín's family, Margarita and her daughter Graciana allegedly screamed insults at the Echaide couple through open windows as the noble couple departed.

9. The surviving trial record reveals basically nothing about Graciana de Olagüe. Other witnesses insisted that the accused witch María Martín de Olagüe—Margarita's daughter and Graciana's sister—was also in her mother's house on Sunday and escaped through a window. See later in this chapter.

The prosecution summary ended with comments on the defendants' whereabouts [fol. 37r]

... It also is hereby noted that the jailer [*alguazil*], in company with Don Pedro de Echaide, both residents of Olague, were in charge of arresting Miguel de Olagüe in the house of [his mother] Margarita de Olagüe. They went there two or three times. Having thoroughly searched the entire house and other houses in the village, Miguel could not be found, nor do people know his whereabouts, nor do they know the whereabouts of [his sisters] Graciana de Olagüe or María Martín de Olagüe.... On account of being guilty, Margarita de Olagüe is being taken as a prisoner [to Pamplona].[10] The constable [Zozaya] is also assigned to prison, and so are Graciana and María Martín in absentia. Their goods and furniture shall be confiscated.

DEFENSE FOR JUAN DE ZOZAYA, OLAGUE'S CONSTABLE

Defense statement from the lawyer for Juan de Zozaya, July 3, 1611 [fol. 39r–v]

Gaspar de Eslava, lawyer for Juan de Zozaya, a resident and constable of Olague.[11] As a plea against the complaint lodged by Don Pedro de Echaide, I intend to prove the following:

First, the parish priest of Olague has a commission from the inquisitor [Alonso de Salazar Frías] who is currently in these mountains. That order warns that no one shall treat anyone as a witch under pain of excommunication. Nor shall anyone speak about witchcraft, nor shall village constables imprison anyone for it. If the opposite occurs, the priest shall notify the inquisitor about it, as witnesses will attest.

... Next, my party has no obligation to imprison, nor can he imprison, anyone without a mandate from a relevant judge, no matter

10. Guilt was presumed in the secular and episcopal legal jurisdictions as well as the inquisitorial one.

11. Gaspar de Eslava had acted as Graciana de Olagüe's lawyer in the defamation case against Miguel de Imbuluzqueta. See chapter 2.

what Doña Graciana de Ursua, wife of the complainant, might say. This is especially true in the case of imprisoning other women and in matters of witchcraft, whose knowledge pertains to the Inquisition.[12]

Next, my party was on the public street of Olague, clearly outdoors, with other residents, on the day and hour that the event occurred, . . . namely, the quarrel and dispute that Doña Graciana de Ursua had with Margarita and Graciana de Olagüe.

Next, my party, Juan de Zozaya, went at once when cries and noise came from inside Margarita de Olagüe's house. My party told the men who were with him to accompany him [beyond the front door], and no one wanted to go, except for Pedro de Olagüe, son of the surgeon. It seemed like a women's quarrel, and thus there was no need for the men to go.[13]

Next, when my party went up to the house, he first found Don Pedro de Echaide with a sword, and Don Pedro was without passion and with sufficient tranquility. Moving ahead, my party saw two of the Echaide servants on either side of Miguel de Olagüe, the young son of Margarita de Olagüe, and the three were handling a drawn knife. My party took the knife and separated them, and put them in peace with one another.[14] In this way, my party calmed down the quarrel, and thus he did what he could and what he was obliged to do as a constable. He told Miguel de Olagüe not to leave the house, and he took everyone else outside. There is no basis for a complaint against my party.

Finally, I beg Your Majesty [the viceroy] to receive information about these details and to view my party as exonerated, without proceeding to prison, . . . and I ask for justice and costs.

Defense witness Juan de Azcarraga, age fifty, July 4, 1611 [fol. 40r]

. . . To the first question, Azcarraga said that what he knows and has seen is that the parish priest of Olague—who has a commission from

---

12. It is crucial to recall that Zozaya was trying to defend himself against charges of dereliction of duty.

13. Another reflection of gender norms and expectations of risk.

14. It was common for male bystanders in Castile and Navarre to break up arguments and fights among men. Taylor, *Honor and Violence.*

the inquisitor [Alonso de Salazar Frías] currently on visitation in the mountains—reported on Sunday, in the parish church and during Mass, that no one should treat anyone as a witch or speak about witchcraft, under pain of excommunication. . . .

Defense witness, Eneko de Ilurdoz, age fifty-four, July 4, 1611 [fol. 40v][15]

. . . To the first question, he said that what he knows and has seen is that the parish priest of Olague—who is said to have a commission from the inquisitor [Alonso de Salazar Frías] currently on visitation in the mountains—warned all the residents of Olague who attended Mass in the parish church that no one should treat anyone as a witch, or treat the subject in any way whatsoever, under pain of excommunication. . . .

Petition from Juan de Zozaya in jail, summer 1611 [fol. 86r]

He has been in prison [in Pamplona] for three days on the demand of Don Pedro de Echaide, because he would not arrest a woman who had irritated Don Pedro. Zozaya had no obligation to arrest that woman: he did not see her commit a crime, nor was there a reason to put him in charge of any imprisonment. He begs Your Majesty [the royal viceroy] to give him complete liberty, so that he may go to his house.

At first, Zozaya was freed but instructed to remain in Pamplona; then, he was given complete liberty.

15. This individual had testified for the Echaide family on June 24, 1611.

PRISON PETITIONS AND DEFENSE WITNESSES FOR
MARGARITA DE OLAGÜE AND HER CHILDREN

Petition from Margarita de Olagüe and two of her children, Miguel de Olagüe and María Martín de Olagüe, from the royal jails, early July 1611 [fol. 48r–v]

They are complaining criminally against Don Pedro de Echaide and Doña Graciana de Ursua, his wife. María Martín is a widow, poor, and a good Christian. Don Pedro went into her room on his own authority, and he gave her many blows with a club, and violently caused her to bleed a great deal from her nose. María Martín fled as well as she could; she went into the street and began to scream, and Don Pedro followed her outside and wanted to beat her again. . . . Don Pedro and his wife put their hands on the women without reason or cause. With the mother [Margarita], they gouged her face and drew blood from it; with the daughter [Graciana] they knocked out a tooth. María Martín ran out the back door and fell into a brook of water that goes behind the house. If Miguel de Olagüe ran into the room, it was to defend his mother and sister. Doña Graciana de Ursua said his mother and sister would be burned as witches.

Defense witnesses for Margarita and María Martín de Olagüe

FEMALE WITNESS MARÍA DE ANZU FOR THE DEFENDANTS,
EARLY JULY 1611 [FOL. 55R]
María Martín de Olagüe is a poor widow . . . who has no reputation of being a witch, and she lives in a quiet way in a tiny house that she has, with four small children. This witness saw María Martín in the street, screaming, "Oh my God, oh my God, I am blameless, people wish me ill because I was born," and wiping her nose with a cloth. This witness talked to her and asked her who did this, and she said Don Pedro [de Echaide]. . . .

CONSTABLE JUAN DE ZOZAYA DEPOSED FOR THE DEFENDANTS
ON JULY 2, 1611 [FOLS. 63R–65V]

... Zozaya is the constable of Olague. He says he will speak the truth,
and we have received an oath from him in the necessary legal form.
He said he is forty-six years old, and he deposed as follows.

To the first question, he said he has known María Martín de
Olagüe, the widow named here, for twenty years. Based on his com-
munications with her, he has held and does hold her as a good Christian, fearful of God and her own conscience, and removed from any
reputation as a witch, although she is poor and has four children.

He says he knows nothing about Questions 2, 3, and 4. To Question 5, he said that what he knows is that he was at the door of his own
house with another resident. Doña Graciana de Ursua, wife of Don
Pedro de Echaide, the accused, came up to him, and taking him by
the arm, said he should go with her and "arrest that good woman," not
saying why, except that this "good woman" was carrying away her children; she did not say where they were being taken. This witness told her
that he could not arrest anyone without a judge's order. Nevertheless,
Doña Graciana told him that he had to arrest this woman, and the two
of them would present her to the inquisitor [Alonso de Salazar Frías].
And this witness kept telling her that he could not arrest the woman
without a judge's order. Talking in this way, they arrived at the door of
the house of Margarita de Olagüe, which is called Mariquirena. This
witness remained at the door while Doña Graciana de Ursua went up
to the house, accompanied by two male and one female servant, and
a daughter of hers.

As soon as they went up, this witness heard a certain noise and
racket: Don Pedro de Echaide had gone up to the rooms of the house
where his wife, Doña Graciana, was.[16] Then María Martín de Olagüe
leaned out the window of the house and asked people on the street
to help them. With all this, this witness went into the house. Then
Graciana de Olagüe also leaned out the window, saying in a loud
voice, "Help, the King! Help, the King!" Hearing this, this witness

16. The trial transcript does not
explain whether Don Pedro was already
in the house when his wife arrived.

said to certain male residents who were with him, that given his duty as constable . . . he would go up and see what was happening, and if necessary, he would call them to come up. He went up, and he only wanted to go into the room where everyone was. He ran into Don Pedro de Echaide, who took him by the arm and said, "What are you doing here, Juan? Nothing is happening." Nevertheless, this witness told Don Pedro to stop and not to leave the house until this witness saw what was going on. . . . And this witness then saw and recognized what was happening, namely, that two male servants of Don Pedro were holding onto Miguel de Olagüe, son of Margarita de Olagüe, and Miguel had a drawn dagger in his hands, and the servants were telling him to drop it and he did not want to. This witness went up to Miguel and took the knife away from him. With this, they all separated, with Don Pedro, Doña Graciana, and their servants going out of the house, and Miguel de Olagüe remaining in it. When she was on the street, Doña Graciana said to Margarita and Graciana de Olagüe, who were at the windows, "These women turned my children into witches," and Margarita and Graciana replied that Doña Graciana herself had done so if anyone had, and not them. Doña Graciana replied, "No, but you did, you're all traitors." With this, Miguel de Olagüe leaned out the window and told Don Pedro de Echaide that if the dagger had succeeded, he would not be eating any more bread and wine.

After things had quieted down, this witness asked Don Pedro de Echaide's daughter, Doña Juana de Echaide, who had been taking her and where. She told him that [the witches] had taken her only one time to the notary's house, and she told him that she did not know who did it. At that, Don Pedro, her father, replied to this witness, "You think she knows who took her?" and with nothing more, they all separated.

When he went up to the room, this witness saw that a male servant of Don Pedro, named Juan de Munuzue, had a bloody hand, and this witness did not know who had hurt him, except that Miguel de Olagüe had a dagger, which he took from him. He also saw that Margarita and Graciana de Olagüe, mother and daughter, had scratched faces, and he does not know who scratched them. Beyond all this, Don Pedro had said in the presence of everyone that the witches had offered his younger son to the Devil to be eaten, cooked and roasted. This is what he knows, nothing more.

Petition from jail, Margarita de Olagüe, summer 1611

She has been a prisoner for eleven days, on account of saying certain words. She is not guilty. If she did say some of them, it was because she was provoked by Don Pedro de Echaide. Without this supplicant having given him any cause, he entered her house with his wife and servants, and mistreated her to the point that she could not speak.[17] [fol. 100r]

... She has been a prisoner for twenty days.... [fol. 105r]

... The court gives her liberty in return for bail, which was delivered by Felipe de Egozcue, from the village of Lantz, on August 4, 1611.... [fol. 116r]

RATIFICATIONS OF WITNESS TESTIMONY FOR THE PROSECUTION

Juan de Olagüe, called Chantoriena, age eleven, September 1611 [fols. 138v–140r]

He swore an oath to speak the truth.[18] He was examined on Saturday in Olague and said he was eleven years old. He knows all the plaintiffs and defendants; he is a first cousin of [María Martín de Olagüe] and a nephew of her mother [Margarita de Olagüe], ... but he nevertheless would speak the truth about what he knows for both sides.... He said that he has been examined another time in this case for Don Pedro Echaide, by a commissioner and jailer whose names he does not know. Before them, he said and deposed the truth and what he knew, and he asked that his first statement be read. Having read it to him in the Basque language, he said it was his first deposition, and what was in it was true, and he ratified and affirmed it.

... And after having been asked in particular about his first deposition, he added to it, and said that he remembered that where

17. Home invasion was an extreme social affront.

18. Theoretically, this boy was too young to swear an oath, being only eleven.

it says in his first deposition that he saw both Echaide children, Don Pedro and Doña Juana, in the *akelarre*, he really only saw the child Don Pedro, and that was one time only, and on the night in question he saw that María Martín de Olagüe, prisoner and cousin of this witness, was carrying the child Don Pedro under her arm. . . . The first time this witness was taken [to the *akelarre*] was the night of the feast of Our Lady this year. And he was taken the first time by his godmother, Margarita de Olagüe, mother of the said prisoner [María Martín de Olagüe], and she took him more than twenty times, up to the day of the Ascension of Our Lord. . . . After that time, María Martín de Olagüe took him [to the *akelarre*] more than ten times.

And a girl of marriageable age, a daughter of the same village, whom he will not name here, took him four nights, the first two when he was sleeping in the kitchen of the Echaide manor, and the next two when he was sleeping in his father's kitchen.[19] He was sleeping in his clothes both times.[20] The girl carried him on her shoulders. For the past forty days the witches have not taken him because he has been in the Echaide manor with the children there, and they keep them awake at night so that they do not sleep, and they sleep during the day, and thus they are guarded. He has been examined in this matter before a commissioner of the Inquisition in the city of Pamplona, and also by the inquisitor [Alonso de Salazar Frías] who has been in Olague and those mountains, to whom he recounted the [same] truth.

There are seventeen older people who go to the *akelarres* of Olague, and only two of them are men. . . . And they have taken many boys and girls of the same age as this witness, as well as younger and older children. In the beginning, he and the other children guarded toads, and the witches told this witness that soon they would make him renounce Christ. . . . All the older witches dance in front of a giant black goat, who is usually seated on a chair. The Goat has three large, black horns. After the dance, they all kiss the Goat under the tail, and

19. The kitchen was the center of Basque households.

20. In 1609, the Suprema had asked the inquisitors to investigate whether children were clothed when witches took them to the Devil's gatherings.

the Goat has sex with the women and also with the men, . . . and when the Goat gets up after the sex, all the witches, men and women, express great sorrow, like someone who has been injured.

Juana de Echaide, older daughter of Don Pedro de Echaide, age eight or nine, September 1611 [fols. 143v–144r]

. . . She says she will speak the truth, and she was not urged to swear an oath, due to being so young. . . . She said that she has previously been examined [on this matter] by a jailer and a commissioner of the city of Pamplona, at the request of her father, . . . where they asked her if she was taken to the *akelarre* and by whom. She told them the truth about what she knows, and who had taken her and how many times. She asked that her previous statement be read to her. And I, the notary, read it, and translated it into the Basque language, and having heard it, she said it was true and ratified it, and that she would say it again if necessary. . . .

She was asked if she has been taken to the *akelarre* since she deposed the first time, and by whom. Adding to her original deposition, she said that after she was examined by the commissioner Sancho de Irurita and the jailer, she was examined on the same matter by the secretary of the inquisitor [Alonso de Salazar Frías] who was in Olague. . . . And last Monday night . . . she was taken to the *akelarre* without her shift, as she had been sleeping in bed. María de Echeberría took her, who is the older daughter of the house of Micheltorena in Olague. She does not know where María took her except that it was all flat, and there in the field María dressed her in a shift of black clothing that she carried with her. María and her mother and a sister of hers were in the *akelarre* with others whom this witness knows from Olague, and they whipped her with some black thorns because this witness had said [to others] that she was taken to the *akelarres*. The same woman who took her, returned her, and the woman tore the black shift to pieces by the time she returned to her parents' house. On the other times she was taken, the witches also dressed the boys and girls whom they had carried nude to the *akelarres*. . . .

OBJECTIONS FROM THE LAWYER FOR THE DEFENSE, JUAN DE URRICOLA, 1611[21] [FOL. 164R–V]

. . . The children of Don Pedro de Echaide and Doña Graciana de Ursua are too young to offer proof, and they are unique witnesses, and they speak on the basis of imaginings and foolish beliefs.[22] The prosecutor's case has rested on seven witnesses: two are the Echaide children, age five and eight, and the other witnesses are under fourteen, except for one who says he is fifteen.[23] At such young ages, they cannot and should not be believed, nor can they offer proof that is convincing.[24] . . . There is no reason to have faith in such statements of children and youngsters, who are easily deceived; they are uttering many nonsensical things that carry no weight and are not likely. . . . The inquisitor [Alonso de Salazar Frías] who has been receiving information about [the witches] has found so many contradictions, delusions, and inconsistencies, along with retractions of depositions, that he has imprisoned no one. Nor has he started a prosecution over what witnesses have said because such a trial would not be well grounded.

The child witches in Olague said that the village priest of Aritzu—one of the most honorable and best Christians in the entire bishopric—was a witch, and that the witches had taken him from his tomb. Later, it was all found to be false. The Royal Court cannot and should not undertake a trial over questions of witchcraft when the matter is based on the statements of children, and thereby torment my party.

Next, Don Pedro de Echaide has pursued my client on account of his children's statements, without any other foundation. My client is a

21. Juan de Urricola was defending Miguel de Imbuluzqueta from charges of slander at the same time. See chapter 2.

22. By "unique," Urricola means that the two children's testimony did not match. Single witnesses could not provide complete proof in any of the three legal jurisdictions in early modern Spain. A complete proof had to consist of two eyewitnesses to the same events or a confession. Single witnesses who attested different events amounted to partial proofs, and no quantity of partial proofs could theoretically amount to a complete proof.

23. It may surprise modern readers to learn that early modern villagers rarely knew their exact ages, and neither did court officials. Discrepancies were common.

24. Contrary to Urricola's statements, the royal secular court in early modern Navarre did treat seriously the legal depositions of children.

poor woman who has no one to look out for her, nor does she have the wherewithal to carry out proofs.[25] Next, in a different episode similar to this one, after many children accused certain people of being witches, their depositions were retracted in our Royal Court. There have been other similar cases in the episcopal court.[26]

RECOMMENDATION FROM THE ROYAL PROSECUTOR AND DON PEDRO ECHAIDE, SEPTEMBER 1611 [FOL. 163R]

Juan de Zozaya was bound to avoid vigilante justice.[27] Margarita de Olagüe told the wife of Don Pedro that she was a wicked witch; she told Don Pedro that he was a known witch, heretic, and traitor. As a witch, María Martín de Olagüe took the plaintiff's children to the Devil's *akelarre*. We ask that they be condemned with the rightful punishments they have brought upon themselves, and may the accused take back the words they have spoken as false and cursed.[28]

TORTURE, A VERDICT, AND PETITIONS

The Royal Court voted to "put María Martín to the question of torture," which means the court wanted to see whether María Martín would

25. Meaning that María Martín de Olagüe had no financial means to carry out the gathering of proof for her own defense. The secular legal jurisdiction did not underwrite the collection of defense testimony.

26. I have not been able to find these legal cases in the royal or episcopal archive in Pamplona.

27. Meaning that the constable Zozaya was bound somehow to have stopped the conflict between the Echaide couple and the witch suspects. Yet he simultaneously was not allowed to involve himself in witchcraft suspicions or accusations, thanks to Inquisitor Salazar's order.

28. Constable Zozaya appears to have been condemned because his refusal to arrest María Martín provoked the Echaide couple into vigilante justice. (There is no evidence that the Echaides themselves were ever prosecuted for their violent attack.) The Royal Court seems to be proceeding as if María Martín had been convicted of witchcraft, although the Spanish Inquisition theoretically had sole legal jurisdiction over witch suspects in this persecution, and the Royal Court's verdict condemned María Martín for defamation; see later in this chapter.

*confess under torture to taking the Echaide children to venerate the
Devil at the akelarres. Transcription of the torture sequence is not
extant in the surviving manuscript, but once the professional torturer
began the process, he judged María Martín unable to withstand it.*

The Royal Court's verdict, September 1611

We condemn Margarita de Olagüe to two years of exile from this city
of Pamplona and from Olague and its lands: she must leave within
six days.[29] For María Martín de Olagüe, the words she spoke are false,
and she must certify this before a notary, and publicly retract them.[30]
Juan de Zozaya must pay fifty pounds to our chamber.

Petitions from Prison from María Martín de Olagüe and her defense lawyer, Juan de Urricola, over the summer and fall of 1611 [fols. 112r, 118r, 122r, 128r–129r, 172r, 174r, 176]

María Martín has been a prisoner for twenty days. Pedro de Echaide
broke down doors and would have killed her if other neighbors had
not arrived. . . .

Juan de Urricola protests the denial of liberty to María Martín.
His party is the aggrieved one in terms of words and deeds. Don Pedro
de Echaide put his hands on her and drew blood. . . .

. . . It has been more than two months, and the supplicant, María
Martín, is still a prisoner. She has been very ill and in constant need
of Doctor Lesaka, the prison physician. And even though he purged
her and had other treatments carried out, she is not better. . . .

---

29. Exile was a routine punishment
in defamation cases.

30. Here, the Royal Court appears
to have thought that María Martín
defamed Don Pedro de Echaide and
his wife, when witnesses indicated that
it was Graciana, María Martín's sister,
who uttered the slurs out the window.
The basis for María Martín's lengthy
prison stay is obscure; she might not
have been able to find anyone willing to
give her bail. The evidence is murky.

. . . She has been in bed for twenty days with a fever, and would have died from hunger if not for [the charity of] the jailer.[31]

. . . November 28, 1611. Maria Martin says it has been more than five months since she was imprisoned, . . . and she was condemned to torture more than three months ago by the court, . . . and afterward, she was very ill in bed. Having been given the Most Holy Sacrament [the Eucharist], she still did not get out of bed. And she is poor and would have nothing to eat if the jailer did not take pity on her.

NEW TESTIMONY ALLOWED, AND MARÍA MARTÍN DE OLAGÜE DIES IN JAIL

In Pamplona, December 13, 1611, . . . the Royal Court admits the legal parties of Juan de Urricola to proof of their injuries . . . to be submitted within a period of fifteen days. . . .

January 10, 1612: Juan de Urricola, lawyer for your royal hearings, says that María Martín de Olague, his client, who has been imprisoned in your royal jails at the request of Don Pedro de Echaide, has died in prison. Urricola asks Your Majesty [the royal viceroy] to carry out the usual examination so that she may be buried.

New Defense

January 11, 1612: Juan de Urricola says that . . . they [sic] have not been able to carry out proof within the fifteen-day deadline because of María Martín's great poverty and other work they had to complete.[32] He begs Your Majesty to order the period of proof extended to thirty days.

31. Prisoners were expected to pay for their own food while in the royal jails. The warden of the royal prison in Pamplona would conduct investigations of prisoners who insisted they had no resources and were starving; those inquiries could take weeks. In María Martín's case, she was classified as requiring charity.

32. Although María Martín died the day before, her defense lawyer is still trying to get witness depositions into evidence.

Defense witness Juan de Alzate, age seventy, January 1612
[fol. 184r–v]

The defendants are known in Olague and the surrounding territory as good Christians, fearful of God and their consciences, without any suspicious kin or lineage of any evil sect, much less witches, until this quarrelsome lawsuit that the Echaide husband has raised. If things were otherwise, this witness would know it. This witness wants to emphasize this fact, because there are certain men and women in this valley and village who, in this witness's memory, have had the reputation of being witches, and that reputation has never left them, although this witness cannot say for certain whether their reputation was accurate. If the defendants and their children had that lineage, the same reputation would apply to them and it would be public knowledge. On the contrary, they have been living with a different reputation, one of Christian people, and of good life and customs.

Margarita de Olagüe is seventy, a widow, and very poor. She [now] has four young grandchildren whom she supports with very great labor and pain. In this village, she has a tiny house and a little land. If she went to live elsewhere [because of the sentence of exile], she would die of hunger, and so would her granddaughters.[33] . . . The Echaide family mistreated both Margarita and her daughter, María Martín, who is now dead.[34] The Echaide husband and his wife are greatly to blame in this matter. . . .

Defense witness Miguel de Oyeregui, age fifty-six,
Olague's woodworker[35] [fols. 184v–185v]

Margarita has four or five young granddaughters whom she supports. Outside of her little house, this witness knows that she has no goods,

33. Pamplona's AGN holds hundreds of secular trials against people who broke sentences of exile and sneaked back into Navarre.

34. The new defense testimony in January 1612 addressed the fates of both Margarita de Olagüe and her dead daughter, María Martín.

35. Miguel de Oyeregui's son, Guillendo, was named as a child witch and testified in the trial of Miguel de Imbuluzqueta; see chapter 2.

furniture, or wherewithal. If the authorities remove her from where she has lived all her life, not only will she die quickly of hunger, but the same will happen to her grandchildren, because they will have no one to assist them. This witness knows them all, and they have no lineage of any evil sect, much less that of witches. If they had such a lineage, this witness would have known about it, but he never heard or understood such a thing until the Echaide husband brought this lawsuit. . . . Rather, Margarita and María Martín had the reputation of gentlewomen [*hidalgas*] on account of never having to pay taxes to anyone: they have been and are completely free of all such charges, except the [indirect taxes] owed to His Majesty the King.[36]

. . . Last June, this witness saw Don Pedro de Echaide and his wife come to Olague from their manor, with two servants and a daughter, in order to hear Mass. Don Pedro and his wife entered the house of Margarita de Olagüe, and Echaide carried his sword in his belt. . . . And this witness went to the house of a neighbor to have lunch. Within a quarter hour of seeing the Echaide couple enter, this witness saw them leave, and this witness suspected that they must have entered to commit some abuse, because it was said that the night or day before, which was Saturday, Echaide had abused María Martín de Olagüe, who is now dead, in her own house. On Sunday, Margarita came to the window with her face very scratched, bloody, and putrid, with some stab wounds, and she told this witness that the Echaide husband, with his people, had abused her in her own house, and she was without fault.[37] This witness was appalled that a gentleman would do such a thing. This witness then saw Margarita at Mass, and she was distraught; it was soon said publicly that the Echaide couple had done it, and that María Martín had been teaching the Echaide children to be witches. If Miguel de Olagüe had not shown up to protect his mother and sister, the abuse would have been much worse.

The very same Sunday, fifteen minutes after all this occurred, this witness went to Mass in Olague, where Pedro de Echaide and his wife

36. The nobility and the clergy in early modern Spain were exempt from paying direct taxes to the Crown. It was entirely possible for Spanish elites to be poor.

37. The adjective here for "putrid" is *podrido*, which in turn is a Spanish translation of the Basque *ustela*.

had also gone. In church, this witness saw the wife's face up close, as well as her hands, but Doña Graciana had no blood anywhere, nor did she appear to have been touched with anything. If she had been, everyone would have known it, and it would have been public knowledge and notorious in the village because there would have been no way to cover it up, and this is the truth.

Defense witness Domingo de Alzate[38] [fol. 186r–v]

... Margarita and the grandchildren will all die of hunger if they move away, because they will be left helpless. . . . This whole business was perceived as very wrong among Olague's residents, not least because Margarita is a widow and poor, and without any protection whatsoever.

Defense witness Juan de Azcarraga [fol. 187r]

... When Echaide, his wife, servants, and children left the women's house, they shouted that the women were witches and had to be burned. And Margarita came to the window with her face completely bloodied, saying that the Echaides had done even worse to her daughter, María Martín. . . .

Defense witness Maria de Olagüe[39] [fols. 188v–189r]

... Margarita and María Martín de Olagüe were known to be gentlewomen; they never paid any [direct] taxes. On that Saturday in June [1611], Don Pedro de Echaide had walked through Olague with a club under his arm, and he was accompanied by the village priest [Pedro de Ortiz] and a student [Don Martín de Unciti], and he called out in the Basque language, "I am going to remove the [evil] spirits from those

38. This witness was Marimartín de Unciti's uncle and María de Alzate's brother; see chapters 2 and 4.

39. This witness is not related to the victims of the Echaide couple.

women who have no soul." There were few people in Olague at the time because they were out weeding cornfields. This witness heard it said that Don Pedro had given María Martín many blows, and this witness went to her house, which was close by, and saw how she had been struck all over her head and shoulders, and her nose was bloody, and she had been very much mistreated. She asked who had done it, and María Martín replied Echaide. Echaide had told María Martín that she was taking his children to the *akelarre*; María Martín told this witness that she was blameless and falsely accused. Therefore, [the next day] María Martín went [for refuge] to the house of Margarita, her mother, where people said she slept, and this is true, and what this witness knows.

. . . This witness said that on Sunday, in the morning, she saw the Echaide husband and wife, with two male servants and a female servant, come down from their manor to Olague, and all of them went into the house of Margarita de Olagüe. Although this witness imagined they must have entered the house to mistreat the women, this witness did not want to leave her own house, but rather sheltered in it. After a while, this witness saw from her door that María Martín, now dead, was bawling and unable to catch her breath, and she had sustained blows, and was soaking wet, and she was saying that when the Echaide husband with his people had gone into the house to kill them, she had jumped through a window out of fear. . . . Then this witness went to Margarita's house, and she saw how the Echaides departed with all their people, leaving Margarita beaten, with her face scratched and putrid, completely bloody, and sobbing.

Besides all this, Echaide's wife said publicly, multiple times, that everyone in Olague was evil, and they were all witches. The Echaide husband said the same.[40] In order not to see or hear any more, this witness went into her own house, and there she found María Martín, trembling, and María Martín remained that way for more than three hours, in her nightdress, without wanting to take even a little broth, or anything else. This witness knows well that the Echaide wife was not maltreated, nor did she appear to have blood on her face or hands. If

---

40. If true, then both Don Pedro and
Doña Graciana committed defamation.

María Martín and Margarita were people who had the wherewithal to complain and litigate, the Echaide couple would be severely punished. It was that much worse for people of their quality to affront honorable people to their faces, with no reason; and to enter a strange house, and hit and maltreat them as much as they had. Undoubtedly, María Martín died in the royal jails from sorrow, and she would have been thirty-four years old, and she left four children without any protection, and this is the truth.

Defense witness Juana de Maya, age fifty-five [fol.189v]

... On Sunday, before Mass, this witness saw the Echaides enter the house: because her home is closest, half a wall apart, she heard them beat and mistreat Margarita. Margarita screamed and her son Miguel came running in from the street. A bit later, the Echaide couple left, saying, "evil, wicked women, all of them," in a loud voice. This witness then left her own house through a window, so they would not see her. After a few minutes, she went to the house of Margarita, and she saw her there crying, with her whole face full of blows, scratched and somewhat bloody. Margarita told this witness that the day before, Saturday, the Echaide husband had beaten and greatly mistreated her daughter, María Martín. And on Sunday, because María Martín was still suffering from that mistreatment, she quickly got out of bed and jumped through the window to the ground below [when she heard the Echaide couple enter her mother's house]. It was a miracle she did not die immediately, because that window was in a high and dangerous place. What Echaide did had been censured in Olague, because what he did was wicked. If the two women had money to spend, they would seriously injure him, but the Echaide family knew that both women were poor and widows, and had nothing to their name. And this witness believes that what Echaide charged the women with doing—taking his daughter and son to the witches' *akelarres*—was false.

Defense witness Madalena de Olagüe, age twenty-two, daughter of Miguel de Oyeregui[41] [fols. 190v–191r]

. . . [On Saturday], this witness heard Echaide say, "For the love of God, before it gets dark, I am going to make someone pay with this club," and the club he was carrying was thick. . . . Then, on Sunday, this witness heard Echaide again, saying, "Where are the wicked witches who have bewitched my daughter?" Because this witness lives half a wall away from Margarita's house, . . . she heard them being beaten and given blows, and Echaide saying, "You wicked witches, here, we dare to kill you."[42] . . . The wife of Echaide said that everyone in Olague was a witch, and this seemed very wrong to this witness, and María Martín did jump out a window out of fear and in her nightdress.

Defense Witness Maria de Olagüe, age seventy, of the house of Micheltorena[43] [fols. 193v–194r]

. . . Margarita and María Martín de Olagüe had no bad reputation at all until the Echaide raised this discord and hatred against them. For this witness, the question of their being witches had no foundation or reason. [It came from] believing children of tender age, who will say whatever they are told for a chestnut.[44] . . . And many children said that witches had taken the village priest of Aritzu out of his tomb because he was [a witch as well], and this man was one of the most

41. Miguel's son, Guillendo, said he was a child witch and reported in court that he was coerced by Juan de Unciti into witchcraft allegations. See chapter 2.

42. This line from Don Pedro—"You wicked witches, here, we dare to kill you"—exemplifies Navarrese frustration with the Spanish Inquisition's relative lack of action until the middle of 1611. When witchcraft accusations accelerated rather than declined after the Inquisition's *auto de fe* in November 1610, multiple villages wrote to the

inquisition tribunal, begging for help with their witch problem. The inquisitors in Logroño refused to act until the Suprema ordered them to carry out a visitation with an edict of grace. Inquisitor Salazar left Logroño with that edict in late May 1611.

43. Juana de Echaide, age eight, named a daughter of this family as a witch in the Imbuluzqueta trial. See chapter 2.

44. In this witch hunt, food was often used as a bribe to entice children into witchcraft accusations.

honored priests in the whole bishopric. The canon Etxalar came [from Pamplona] and made them open the tomb where the priest had been buried, in front of many people, and what they found there was just the same as when they originally buried him.[45] This witness saw both his original burial and his exhumation. The story about the witches taking him was completely false.

. . . Saturday, she was walking to her daughter's house, and she ran into María Martín, now dead, who was standing next to a door, crying, bruised all over her shoulders and head, and with her face bloodied. Seeing her in such bad shape, she asked who had mistreated her, and she responded that it was Pedro de Echaide, and she did not know know why. As this witness walked on, she saw Don Pedro de Echaide with the club in his hand, and the village priest [Pedro de Ortiz] with him. She told them there was enough justice for everyone, and no one should take justice into his own hands. It was a wicked deed to treat such an honorable woman [María Martín] in such a way: she was poor and a widow, and mistreating her was not well done.[46] Don Pedro replied that María Martín had made witches out of his children, and since there had been no justice, he had to take matters into his own hands. With that, they separated.[47]

On July 16, 1612, the Royal Court reiterated its sentence against Margarita de Olagüe, stipulating that she must go into exile and pay costs.

---

45. A canon of a cathedral was a cleric who received a yearly stipend from that church and who participated in the cathedral's governance.

46. This resident, who perhaps had claims to wealth and status, was not afraid to chastise Don Pedro and Olague's priest in pubic and to their faces. Note, however, that she did not insult them.

47. That excuse—that justice had not been done—was used everywhere in Navarre to warrant the local torture of witch suspects in this persecution.

DEFENSE OBJECTIONS AND NEW DEVELOPMENTS

Legal protests from Margarita's lawyer, Juan de Urricola, July 1612 [fols. 207r, 208r, 209r]

. . . The defendant is more than eighty years old. She has no one to look after her, nor can she follow [her] children.[48]

. . . The defendant cannot pay costs; the plaintiff has not even presented a list of costs. It is publicly known that Don Pedro was living in his sister's house [while the case was ongoing], and hence he cannot claim those expenses as costs. . . .

. . . The defendant [Margarita] is not leaving [on exile], in contempt and violation of the court's sentences. . . .

A reprieve from the Royal Court, July 28, 1612 [fol. 213r]

Regarding the demand from Don Pedro de Echaide and his attorney, which asks that Margarita de Olagüe leave to complete the penalty of exile given to her, and other matters. The Royal Court gives Margarita de Olagüe freedom not to leave to complete said exile until her countersuit against Pedro de Echaide is resolved. This order is so declared with the signatures of Dr. Sanlizente, regent [of the viceroy], Licentiate Ledena, Doctors Oco and Buruete, and Licentiate Fermin of the Royal Council.

48. Although the first statement of Margarita's countersuit included the name of her son, Miguel, it appears that charges against him were abandoned. There is no evidence that Margarita's other daughter, Graciana, was ever taken into custody. The lawyer's claim here that Margarita "cannot follow her children" might reflect the fact that Miguel and Graciana successfully fled Olague.

CHAPTER 4

Mother and Daughter

Some figures in Olague turned the witch hunt into an opportunity to ruin their spouses.[1] Olague's blacksmith, Juan de Unciti, was married for a second time to María de Alzate, who also had been married before. Unciti and Alzate had a daughter together—Marimartín de Unciti—who was twelve or thirteen years old in the summer of 1611.[2] Unciti had at least one son from a prior marriage, Martín de Unciti, who was twenty-three in 1611 and who had risen to the position of deacon in the Catholic Church. Juan de Unciti and María de Alzate's union was dire, to the point that they separated in 1609: he continued to live in Olague, while she and their daughter moved to Lantz. Nevertheless, the bishop of Pamplona believed married couples should live together, in accordance with the sacrament of marriage as laid out in the decrees of the Council of Trent (1545–63).[3] When one of the bishop's officials learned that María and Juan were living apart, he ordered them to cohabitate once more. Since María was the one who had moved out, the church threatened her with excommunication if she did not obey. María and Marimartín returned to Olague around January 1611.

At some point between late March and June 1611, Marimartín publicly and repeatedly named herself and her mother as witches. But she also testified in the two slander trials excerpted in chapters 2 and 3, and her legal depositions could not have been more different. In her first deposition, given in June 1611, she testified for the plaintiff,

1. Most of the material in this chapter comes from a dossier in Pamplona's diocesan archive: ADP, C/1.232, n. 38.

2. It was rare for illiterate villagers to know exactly how old they were, which is why they deposed in court that they were "more or less" a particular age.

3. For the intersections between Trent's values and decrees and this witch persecution, see Homza, *Village Infernos*, 51–61.

Don Pedro de Echaide: she said she was a child witch and named her mother and María Martín de Olagüe as witches in sentences that lacked all detail. A month later, in July 1611, Marimartín testified for Miguel de Imbuluzqueta's defense: at that point, she deposed for entire folios about the intimidation inflicted on her by her father and other relatives to make false accusations. Marimartín ended up telling residents of Olague what she had endured; there is no doubt that the coercion she suffered was made public. In August 1611, Marimartín's mother, María de Alzate, took her to Pamplona and installed her as a servant; when the Royal Court went looking for Marimartín in September 1611 to ratify the testimony she had given in the Echaide trial, they could not find her because her mother had put her into hiding. In late 1611, when the bishop of Pamplona again ordered María to resume living with Juan de Unciti, she filed a petition for separation with the bishop's court. Her petition was granted.

SOME IMPORTANT CHARACTERS, IN ORDER OF APPEARANCE

Marimartín de Unciti, age twelve or thirteen, daughter of María de Alzate and Juan de Unciti and stepsister to Don Martín de Unciti, a deacon in the Catholic Church

Don Pedro de Echaide, a nobleman and the plaintiff in chapter 3, married to Doña Graciana de Ursua, and father to Pedro de Echaide and Juana de Echaide, child witches.

Juan de Unciti, Olague's blacksmith, husband of María de Alzate, father of Marimartín de Alzate and Don Martín de Unciti, first cousin to Olague's parish priest, Pedro de Ortiz, and Graciana de Olagüe

María de Alzate, wife of Juan de Unciti, mother of Marimartín de Alzate and stepmother of Don Martín de Unciti, sister of Domingo de Alzate

Pedro de Echaide, child witch, young son of Don Pedro de Echaide

Juana de Echaide, child witch, young daughter of Don Pedro de Echaide

Miguel de Imbuluzqueta, alleged witch in chapter 2

Don Martín de Unciti, age twenty-three, deacon, son of Juan
    de Unciti, stepson of María de Alzate, and stepbrother of
    Marimartín de Unciti
Graciana de Olagüe, plaintiff against Miguel de Imbuluzqueta in
    chapter 2, first cousin of Juan de Unciti and Pedro de Ortiz
Pedro de Ortiz, Olague's parish priest and first cousin of Juan de
    Unciti and Graciana de Olagüe
Don García de Olagüe, parish priest of the village of Aritzu, who
    cured María de Alzate's broken arm and whose body was
    allegedly cannibalized by Olague's witches.
Domingo de Alzate, brother of María de Alzate and uncle to
    Marimartín de Unciti

MARIMARTÍN DE UNCITI'S TESTIMONY FOR PLAINTIFF
DON PEDRO DE ECHAIDE IN HIS DEFAMATION CASE
AGAINST MARGARITA AND MARÍA MARTÍN DE OLAGÜE,
JUNE 24, 1611[4]

This witness is the daughter of Juan de Unciti, the blacksmith. She says
she is thirteen years old, more or less, on account of which we are not
receiving an oath from her.[5] Without the oath, she [still] offered to
speak the truth and deposed as follows. María de Alzate, her mother,
has taken her to the *akelarre* where the witches hold their gatherings.
After her mother did that, María de Elizondo, called Aguillarenci, took
her three times to the *akelarres*.[6] And there she has seen Pedro and
Juana de Echaide, children of the plaintiff, Don Pedro de Echaide. It
was María Martín de Olagüe who carried Pedro and Juana away, and
this witness has seen her many times in the *akelarre*, and her being a
witch is very well-known in Olague: it is public and notorious.[7] This

4. AGN, *Tribunales reales*, #41366,
fol. 9v.
    5. At that age, Marimartín should
have sworn an oath to tell the truth.
She gave variable ages for herself in her
legal depositions.
    6. The surviving evidence does not
relay anything about this individual.

7. María Martín de Olagüe had
been attacked in her home as a witch
by Don Pedro de Echaide. On his
demand, she was thrown into the royal
jail in Pamplona in June 1611 and died
there in January 1612. See chapter 3.

is what the witness knows and can say to the question, and it is the truth. Having read her statement back to her, she ratified and affirmed it, and she did not sign because she did not know how to write.

MARIMARTÍN DE UNCITI'S TESTIMONY FOR DEFENDANT MIGUEL DE IMBULUZQUETA, JULY 8, 1611[8]

This witness is the daughter of Juan de Unciti, the blacksmith. This witness is twelve. What she remembers is that after the Feast of the Resurrection this year, a servant of her father, along with Don Martín de Unciti, her [step]brother, took her to the house of Graciana de Olagüe, the widow and the opposing party.[9] She did not know why they took her there. Graciana was in the house and a son of Graciana was there too, named Sancho. Her [step]brother Martín de Unciti and her father's servant began to chat [*charlar*] about the witches they said Olague had. Turning to this witness, they told her that she was one too, because the children who said they were witches had seen her with her mother in the *akelarres*. And she had to confess and to say what happened, and who took her, and which adults in Olague were witches. Not ever having heard that rumor, this witness said and repeated multiple times that she was not a witch and she did not know who was, and it was not true. . . . Then, Graciana and her son, with great severity, sometimes one, and sometimes the other, told her not to deny it and to confess the truth.[10] Many persons who were adults had declared that this witness was a witch, and so was her mother. . . .

Then, all of them with one voice, threats, and compulsion, told her that whether she wanted to or not, she had to declare and say in their presence, before leaving the house, that she and her mother and the other persons they named were witches. Sancho [Graciana's son] spoke for all of them in assuring her that it would not be difficult for

8. AGN, *Tribunales reales*, #330569, fols. 95r–98r.

9. Marimartín never told the royal secular court that Don Martín de Unciti was actually her stepbrother, but her mother did. See chapter 2.

10. We can presume that Sancho's testimony about being a witch himself, which he gave in the trial of Miguel de Imbuluzqueta, was false.

Olague's priest [Pedro de Ortiz] to have her burned as a *negativa*.[11] If she confessed, she would remain free like the rest. She felt so much the persistency that Graciana de Olagüe and her son Sancho made in this demand, combined with her [step]brother Don Martín de Unciti, and her father's servant, that they carried her to the edge of truth. The compulsion and threats that they turned on her, and the persuasive methods they used, were so great that her free will was disturbed, and they forced her from the truth and made her say that she was a witch, and so was her mother, along with Miguel de Imbuluzqueta and his wife, and all the rest she had named. . . . And then, they told her she had to say the same outside the house.[12] After this happened, they set her free from Graciana's house. . . . And Graciana and the rest were very happy with having succeeded in their intention.

The next day, and for many thereafter, Don Martín de Unciti on his part, and her father's servant on his part, caught her alone and warned her not to vary one iota from what she had said and declared in Graciana's house. If she disobeyed, they promised her that they would tie her around the throat with some cords and throw her over the dam.[13] . . . She was charged by the priest [Don Pedro Ortiz] as well, so that she said and publicized many days that she was a witch when people asked. She also said her mother, María de Alzate, and Miguel Imbuluzqueta and his wife and one of his sons, named Pedroco, were witches. . . . And she did not stop there, but being taken before Dr. Muñariz [in Pamplona], she said the same things, being persuaded by her [step]brother, Don Martín de Unciti, who accompanied her.

. . . Afterward, on another day, when Licentiate Acosta was in the village, she was taken before him by Olague's priest and Don Pedro de Echaide, who owns the manor of Echaide, so that she would say the same things. The priest and Don Pedro charged her very much to do so, and so she did. But afterward, she fell into contemplating the offense

11. The group was summoning the memory of the Inquisition's November 1610 *auto de fe*, when eleven individuals were burned at the stake.

12. There is no evidence that Marimartín named Miguel de Imbuluzqueta and members of his family as witches in a legal deposition, though she may well have done so publicly.

13. Bodies of water were everywhere in Navarre, and experts believe that no one there in the early modern period knew how to swim. Drowning was a real possibility.

and enormous injury she [had committed] toward her mother, Miguel de Imbuluzqueta, and all the other honorable people of the village, through lies and against all truth.[14] And she has [already] declared it and confessed it [publicly], as she now declares and confesses in her deposition, under charge of the oath she has sworn, and the account she will have to give to God.[15] Everything she has said and declared publicly against her mother and the family of Miguel de Imbuluzqueta . . . and all the other persons . . . has been and is false and deceitful, against all truth. She did it on account of the force and violence, terrors and threats made against her by Graciana de Olagüe and her son, and her [step]brother Martín de Unciti, and her father's servant. . . . She has never been taken to the *akelarre* or gatherings of witches by anyone, either from this village or outside of it, . . . and she does not know what a witch is.

Besides all this, the witness now has to say how, eight days ago, a little more or less, two commissioners of the Inquisition came to Olague. That afternoon they had this witness brought to their house, where they interrogated her to say what she knew and had seen concerning the witches found in Olague; they told her she should name each of them. From beginning to end, this witness told them everything she has said in this deposition, under the questioning and requestioning that they conducted.

. . . A little while after [the inquisition commissioners' interrogation of her], the village priest [Pedro de Ortiz] called to her; he was in company with Juan de Unciti and Don Martín de Unciti, her father and [step]brother.[16] The priest was angry: he accused her of not having said and confessed before the inquisition commissioners what she had earlier stated against herself, her mother, and other persons.[17]

14. Chapter 1 contains identical examples of self-reflection over false testimony, when child witches confessed before inquisitors or their employees and then retracted their earlier statements.

15. Marimartín had previously admitted to falsely accusing her mother of witchcraft before her mother and other adults; see chapter 2. Adults and children who falsely named themselves as witches and then accused others frequently experienced profound despair over what they had done.

16. Pedro de Ortiz, Olague's priest, was Juan de Unciti's first cousin.

17. This comment by Ortiz points to some sort of malfeasance by the inquisition commissioners or their staff, since Marimartín's depositions before them should have been kept secret.

Whereupon this witness replied that all her [previous] statements were lies, obtained through compulsion and violence, against all truth, and she knew how to recant. When he heard this, the priest raised his hand, gave her a very hard slap in the face, and knocked her down, saying, "You wicked pig, if you don't say the same as you did before, I'll have to rip out your guts by the handful." Juan de Unciti and Don Martín de Unciti likewise told her that if she did not go back to saying what she had before, they would later embrace her in her death shroud. They said it in such a way that this witness began to tremble, and she was dazed. To escape the anger of the priest and her father and [step] brother, she promised them that she would say as much as they wanted before the inquisition commissioners. When she placated them in this way, they charged her to do exactly that.

The following day, in the morning, they took her there again. She told the inquisition commissioners what had happened the previous day, which was why she could say nothing in the new interview.[18] The commissioners asked her whether she had told the truth in what she had told them the day before. And even though the commissioners questioned her all over again, she was firm in saying and declaring the truth and nothing more, which is everything she has declared in this deposition. Today, a boy named Miguel told her that even though she had said nothing before the Inquisition's commissioners, he and other children had declared who were witches in Olague, and the village priest [Pedro de Ortiz] had promised that he would award them the witches' estates once the witches were burned, . . . and this is the truth.[19]

18. In her second interview with the commissioners, Marimartín told them about her relatives' abuse and refused to repeat witchcraft accusations, though she had told those relatives she would do so.

19. Of course, the priest Pedro de Ortiz had no legal rights at all to take possession of other people's property upon their deaths, unless they had explicitly willed it to him in last testaments; no evidence to that effect has been found. The theme of burning was constant in legal testimony from Olague; the Inquisition's death sentences in November 1610 had made an impression.

MARITAL SEPARATION

On December 1, 1611, Marimartín's mother, María de Alzate, filed a
formal petition for marital separation from Juan de Unciti with the
episcopal court in Pamplona.

Statement by María de Alzate's lawyer, December 10, 1611, regarding her petition for a marital separation [fol. 1r][20]

. . . María de Alzate's first husband died eleven years ago, . . . and for
many years, without provocation, her current husband [Juan de Unciti]
mistreated her by word and deed many times, without a reason or
cause that could be just. He has put violent hands on her. Eight years
ago, he broke her left arm with a blow from an iron fire shovel; Don
García de Olagüe, village priest of Aritzu, now dead, cured her.[21]
Juan de Unciti has often hit her in the face and drawn a great deal of
blood. Not being content with this, at the same time, he threw her out
of the house, and also threw out a son and a daughter of hers from
her first marriage.[22] He was compelled to take her back after she had
lived in the village of Lantz for two years without complaint. . . . By
order of the episcopal vicar, she returned to the house and company
of her husband, with whom she lived with much trouble on account
of the mistreatment that he gave her. They only slept together very
infrequently.[23]

[Their renewed cohabitation] went on for eight months, a little
more or less, until María de Alzate left Juan de Unciti's house, being
unable to live with him.[24] [She also left] because he broadcast it about

---

20. ADP, C/1.232, n. 38.

21. This was the dead priest whom
the Olague child witches insisted had
been cannibalized by witches and
whose relatives exhumed his body. See
chapter 2.

22. None of the witnesses for either
side confirmed that children from
María's first marriage were thrown out
of Juan de Unciti's house.

23. This sequence of points was
repeated elsewhere: it seems that Juan
de Unciti's refusal to sleep with María
was interpreted as another sign of his
hatred for her.

24. Thus, María de Alzate moved
out of Juan de Unciti's house in August
1611.

that she was a witch, when the truth was otherwise. Since that time, she has lived and does live in the house of her brother, Domingo de Alzate [in Olague]. Now it appears that the episcopal visitor of this diocese, Dr. Luís Venegas y Figueroa, ordered in his most recent visitation that she and Juan de Unciti should live together [again] under pain of excommunication.[25] For these reasons, and others that will be declared in this trial, she should not be compelled to live with her husband, because it is certain that he would kill her if he had the means.

Response from the lawyer of Juan de Unciti, December 1611
[fol. 7r–v]

María de Alzate's petition asks for marital separation and food [alimentos], and that she be allowed to attend ecclesiastical services.

His party [Juan de Unciti] and the opposing party [María de Alzate] have been married for twelve or thirteen years, more or less. In all the time they have lived together in Unciti's house, he has never mistreated her or broken her arm, or anything else. . . . But rather, he always treated her well with deeds and words.

It is also true that without cause and on her own authority, she left the house [during the marriage] four or five times to enjoy her liberty, and she has walked in this city [Pamplona] and other places, where she was seen.[26] Through the assistance of other people, she was taken back into Unciti's house, as is notorious. And she was also taken back because the bishop's visitors ordered as much when they were in this village. Juan de Unciti was not obliged to take her back, but he has taken her back every time she left in order to serve God. In the same manner, without cause, she has now left again and is missing, and my party told her not to go when she wanted to leave, and he told her what she had done before was enough, and not to provoke more dishonor. Nevertheless, she left and is now outside my party's house. . . .

25. This episcopal visitor could well be a relative of Pamplona's bishop at the time, Alonso Venegas y Figueroa.

26. Married women who left their homes to walk at leisure were violating gender norms. María de Alzate's offense was that much greater for having walked alone in Pamplona, a city.

Without intending to insult her, the contrary party [María de Alzate] has been and is a woman with a wicked tongue and is very foul-mouthed. She habitually loses the respect due to my party, who is her husband, as well as to the children of his first marriage, saying many evil and insulting words to them without cause, and without taking into consideration that one of those children, named Don Martín [de Unciti], is an ordained deacon. In order to avoid any harm, my party and all his children put up with her and do not respond to what she says, as is notorious.

Given that my party has a good and peaceful character, he has never mistreated her or her children, nor did he ever mistreat his first wife or their children.

The contrary party has removed the daughter [Marimartín] from this [second] marriage on her own authority, against the wishes of my party. For the four months that the daughter has been gone, my party has tried to bring her to his house, and the contrary party has not desired it and has blocked it to the best of her ability.[27]

. . . The contrary party came to my party with nothing, not even a dowry. . . . My party has never called the contrary party a witch, although many others have. . . . And information about this has been received by the Spanish Inquisition.[28]

Response from María de Alzate's lawyer, December 1611
[fols. 9r–10r]

The bishop's representative ordered María de Alzate back to marital life with Juan de Unciti, her husband, and when she did not comply with the order, she was prohibited from hearing the divine offices.[29] That order has been appealed to Your Lordship [the bishop], given her reasons for not wishing to make a marital life with her husband;

27. María de Alzate placed her daughter, Marimartín, in hiding in August 1611.

28. This statement is true, to the extent that inquisition commissioners and Inquisitor Salazar visited Olague

in 1611 and heard the village's witches identified.

29. Meaning that María de Alzate could not attend religious services in the parish church.

there is a pending lawsuit over it. Your Lordship originally ordered that she should not be prohibited from hearing the divine offices for fifteen days, but that permission will soon expire. I beg Your Lordship to extend the period during which she can hear the divine offices for the extent of this lawsuit, or until Your Lordship sees fit, and I ask for justice.

. . . No matter what Juan de Unciti's lawyer says, the case must be decided as my party asked in her petition of December 1, which I reproduce here. It must be ordered that there be a separation of house and cohabitation for the reasons contained in the enclosed petitions. Juan de Unciti has tried many times to have María de Alzate accused as a witch—inducing one of his daughters to say it, and even threatening that daughter—and he himself has been publicizing and saying as much to various people. From his actions, it can be deduced how little marital love he has for María de Alzate; rather, he has hatred and notorious ill will toward her. His hatred and ill will imply that she is in evident danger of her life, and of losing her life in the house and cohabitation of her husband. Thus I ask and beg Your Lordship that despite what the contrary party alleges, may Your Lordship declare that my party not be compelled to comply with the visitor's order [of renewed cohabitation]. . . . I ask for justice and costs.

Questions for María de Alzate's witnesses in her petition for marital separation, December 1611 [fol. 12r]

Do they know that twelve years ago, when she was widowed through the death of Juan de Aritzu, her first husband, she then married Juan de Unciti, with whom she had a daughter, now aged eleven.[30]

Do they know that the contrary party [Juan de Unciti] has mistreated my party for many years without reasonable cause, putting hands on her person. Moreover, he wanted to damage her reputation with insulting words that he said publicly about her, when those words did not fit and were foreign to her good life and conversation.

30. No one in the various legal documents knew exactly how old Marimartín was, and she did not, either.

Eight years ago, the contrary party broke my party's left arm with a blow from an iron coal shovel, without her having given him any occasion for it that would excuse it, as witnesses will attest. The witnesses will say how the village priest of Aritzu cured her injury, and how the contrary party threw her out of the house, along with the children of her first marriage.

[The witnesses will say] that many, many times over [the past] eight years, the contrary party gave my party many slaps in the face with an open palm, as well as blows on her body with a closed fist. [He also hit her] with clubs and other things, whereby he made her vomit blood.[31]

After he threw her out of the house, my party lived in Lantz in her own house with her son and daughter for two years, continuously, without the contrary party making a fuss about it.[32] At the end of that time [around January 1611], by order of the episcopal visitor, my party returned to the house and company of her husband, the contrary party, and she lived with him with great adversity because of the evil treatment he gave her, and they did not sleep in the same bed. The witnesses will say what they know, and if they have heard it said publicly that my party is a witch, and that the contrary party threatened his own daughter to say my party is a witch.

Witnesses who testified in January 1612 for María de Alzate

MARÍA DE OLAGÜE, WIDOW, AGE FORTY-EIGHT, WIFE OF ADAM DE ESAIRI [FOLS. 17R–18V]
She knows both parties and is related to them, though in a distant degree. She will nevertheless speak only the truth.

. . . She knows they were married; her house is adjacent to theirs. She heard María de Alzate complain many times, day and night, about

31. Hitting someone with a closed fist was a much more serious offense than a slap with an open palm. Drawing blood increased the seriousness of an attack.

32. Elsewhere in the petition, María de Alzate is said to have had one son and one daughter from her first marriage. We can presume that the daughter here is Marimartín, from the second marriage.

how her husband mistreated her and put his hands on her. . . . And this witness saw María de Alzate with signs and injuries of blows on her face as well as her body. . . . She saw the broken arm in a sling and asked what had happened. María de Alzate replied, "Something bad," although this witness understood that Alzate's husband had broken her arm. Alzate spent a long time with her arm in a sling, and after a few days, the parish priest of Aritzu, now dead, cured it.

BRIGIDA DE ARITZU, WIFE OF MIGUEL DE OLAGÜE, AGE TWENTY-EIGHT, OF THE HOUSE OF BARBERENACHEA [FOLS. 18R–19V]
. . . She was a servant for the parish priest of Aritzu. One day—she cannot remember when—María de Alzate came to Aritzu with her arm in a sling, so that the priest could cure it. When the priest saw her, he realized she had a broken arm. Asking her how this misfortune had happened, Alzate said in this witness's presence that her husband had done it with a blow from the coal shovel. The priest cured Alzate in a few days. This witness often heard that when the two were living together, he always gave her a miserable life and mistreated her, putting hands on her, and so they did not live together. . . .

MARÍA DE OLAGÜE, WIFE OF JUAN DE ASCARRAGA, AGE THIRTY-TWO[33] [FOLS. 20V–21R]
This witness currently lives in a house attached to the one of Juan de Unciti, and she did so while Unciti and Alzate were living together. Many different times she perceived how Juan de Unciti gave María, his wife, a miserable life, speaking badly to her and putting hands on her, giving her blows on her face to the point that signs were seen. . . . When she heard that he was mistreating her, this witness left her house and separated them. This witness never saw any reason whatsoever for him to mistreat his wife in these ways, but rather she held her as an honorable, retiring, and industrious woman. This witness saw that María had her arm in a sling: when she asked what had happened, María said her husband had hit her. Once, upon leaving her house she

---

33. Juan de Ascarraga was one of the adults who heard Marimartín de Olague despair over her witchcraft confession and accusation. See chapter 2.

realized that Unciti was mistreating his wife because she saw María was walking around without her headdress, with her hair loose, and Unciti had knocked off the headdress.[34]

JUAN DE IRURITA, SERVANT OF JUAN DE ZOZAYA, AGE TWENTY-EIGHT [FOLS. 21R–22R]

Six years ago [in 1606], he was a servant of Juan de Unciti, who employed him for three years. He saw Unciti mistreat his wife very badly and without cause. Twice Unciti put his hands on her, and other times, when he wanted to manhandle her, this witness prevented him from doing so because she is an honorable, industrious, and retiring woman. Unciti was accustomed to give his wife a miserable life, without respecting her as his wife. . . .

He remembers that once, because she reacted to something Unciti said, Unciti grabbed the coal shovel that was in the kitchen and hit her left arm with it. . . . And he heard her say two or three times that she left the house because she hated the miserable life Unciti gave her and could not live with him.

MAGDALENA DE OLAGÜE, SINGLE WOMAN, AGE TWENTY-THREE, DAUGHTER OF MIGUEL DE OYEREGUI, THE WOODWORKER[35] [FOLS. 23V–24R]

. . . She knows Marimartín by sight and conversation that she has had and does have with her, and that is publicly known. She has seen her brought up and fed, and Marimartín is the legitimate daughter of the two parties, and is about eleven years old.

This witness lives in her parents' house, which faces the house of the two parties. Many different times, Juan de Unciti has given María de Alzate a miserable life, treating her very badly with words as if she were a stranger, rather than esteeming her as his wife. He has given her blows in the face and other parts of her body, and knocked off her

---

34. In the early modern period, the headdresses of Basque women looked like wrapped towels. Legal sources often describe those women as surviving physical attacks because of their headdresses. Knocking off a headdress was akin to knocking off a man's hat; it was a serious affront to personal honor.

35. Miguel de Oyeregui's son, Guillendo, falsely confessed to being a witch and deeply regretted accusing others. See chapter 2.

headdress, causing a very great scandal in the neighborhood. Many times, this witness saw that when Juan de Unciti wanted to hurt María, she fled from him and escaped, and went to the house of this witness's parents, and to other houses in the neighborhood. María cried and complained about the miserable life her husband gave her, without cause or reason for him to do it. . . .

She heard from María and others that her husband did not sleep with her, nor did he want to, but only with whomever he wanted.[36]

MARTÍN DE LANTZ, IRONWORKER FROM LANTZ, AGE TWENTY-FOUR [FOLS. 25V–26V]

. . . Two years ago [1610], he was a servant to Juan de Unciti in Olague, working in the profession of blacksmith for a period of fifteen months. . . . María de Alzate is industrious, quiet, and obedient, and Juan de Unciti, her husband, treated her very badly with words. This witness and others in Unciti's house stopped him when he wanted to put his hands on María, getting in between Unciti and his wife. In the end, Unciti treated her as if she were a woman of evil reputation, demonstrating in everything he did that he wished her ill, without this witness ever having seen anything that could be the cause of such maltreatment. Instead, this witness saw María serve her husband with much goodwill, punctuality, and helpfulness, like a good and honorable woman. In matters of the household, Unciti did not allow her to take a hand in anything, as if he did not know her, nor did he allow her to sit at the table at the time they usually ate.[37] When they ate, Unciti gave her bread from his hand as if she were a servant. Many times this witness saw that her husband would not even give her cold meat, and he and his companions gave her what they had to eat from their plates. She was heartbroken over it.

36. For a witness who reported that she had Juan de Unciti's child after he was married to María de Alzate, see later in this chapter.

37. Such treatment would have been an extreme affront.

Questions for Juan de Unciti's witnesses [fol. 28r–v]

Do they know that Juan de Unciti and María de Alzate have been married for twelve or thirteen years.

Do they know that Unciti never mistreated Alzate. There was no broken arm; she was always treated well.

Do they know that María de Alzate has left Unciti's house of her own free will and has gone walking throughout this city [of Pamplona] and other places.

Do they know that Unciti took her back, although he was not obliged to do so.

Not intending to defame her, do they know that she has been and is a woman of evil speech and very foul-mouthed, and disrespectful to Unciti and his children.

Do they know that Unciti has a good and peaceful temperament, and has never mistreated her.

Do they know that she brought no goods whatsoever to the marriage.

Defense witnesses for Juan de Unciti, who testified in January 1612

JUAN DE OLAGÜE, A YOUTH, SERVANT OF JUAN DE UNCITI,
AGE TWENTY-ONE [FOLS. 30R–31R]

He is Juan de Unciti's nephew; his father and Juan de Unciti are brothers, and he is also the cousin of Marimartín. He has been working as a blacksmith for four or five months. Juan de Unciti always treated María de Alzate well, eating at one table, sleeping in one bed on occasions when she wanted to.[38] He does not recall the particular day, but she left the house, and her husband said to her, "What ideas and madness have gotten hold of you to walk around in such a way? What happened in the past is enough. Stay in the house, and don't give anyone the opportunity to perceive your whims and madness." Nevertheless,

---

38. The phrase about the sexual contact is "dormiendo en una cama las veces que era su voluntad," which I am interpreting as her desire to have sex, not Unciti's.

María de Alzate left with her bed and lived elsewhere thereafter. . . .
This witness has never heard Juan de Unciti call his wife a witch, but
he has heard children of Olague say several times that she is one.

MARÍA DE OLAGÜE, WIFE OF JUAN DE ETULAÍN, AGE FORTY

[FOL. 33R–V]

She is not related to the two parties, except that she and Juan de Unciti
had a child ten years ago in this village. She would still speak the truth.
. . . She has seen María de Alzate leave the house two or three times
on her own initiative, and she has been taken back by Unciti through
the intercession of other people. . . . Her own house is nearly opposite
to theirs, and she has seen María be insolent with her husband and
with his children from his first marriage, having quarrels and fights.
. . . Juan de Unciti lived very well with his first wife. . . . María de Alzate
took the daughter [Marimartín] away, and even though her father
wanted to take the daughter back, the mother did not want to bring
her back. The daughter [Marimartín] of Juan de Unciti and María
de Alzate told this witness that her mother was a witch, though this
witness cannot remember the exact day; this witness reprehended the
daughter to watch what she was saying, and the daughter returned to
saying that it was true.

JUAN DE IRIONDO, AGE THIRTY [FOLS. 35R–36R][39]

. . . He used to live in a house that was in front of Juan de Unciti's,
and during that time (it might have been eight years ago), Unciti and
Alzate got along just fine. . . . He does not remember the specific day,
but he saw Maria de Alzate at the door of her husband's house, with
the village constable [jurado]. And Alzate asked her husband for her
bed, and he replied that her bed was in the house and he was not
going to do anything about it. If she did not want to be with him, she
should take the bed. As soon as she took the bed, she carried it away,
wherever it suited her. . . . Various times this witness has heard Juan
de Unciti's daughter [Marimartín] say that her mother was a witch,

39. Iriondo was identified as being
present with Don Pedro de Echaide
in multiple interactions with Olague's

child witches, as well as with the
accused witch Miguel de Imbuluzqueta. See chapters 2–3.

and that her mother took her to the *akelarre* and made her a witch. This is what he knows as to the question.

BERNARD DE ORGUI, NATIVE OF BAYONNE IN THE KINGDOM OF FRANCE, AGE TWENTY-FOUR, WHO CURRENTLY RESIDES IN THE VILLAGE OF ZUBIRI [FOL. 36R–V]

He was a servant and an apprentice for four or five years to Juan de Unciti. He left Unciti's employment and house three years ago. When he was there, this witness saw that Unciti did not esteem his wife, as if she was not part of his house or had anything to do with it.[40] Unciti took no more notice of her than if he did not know her, and he gave her a miserable life, treating her badly with words and putting hands on her person, giving her blows in the face that left signs. Seeing the miserable life Unciti gave her and the evil way he treated her, many times this witness got between the two of them and made Unciti leave her alone, so that vigilante justice would not occur. Unciti only slept with her on rare occasions. And María de Alzate was upset by the little confidence that Unciti had in her and the miserable life he gave her, and this witness did not see in Alzate any reason or occasion to treat her in such fashion. She is an honorable, good, industrious woman who was capable of answering back on more than a few occasions to defend herself, and this is the truth.

PEDRO DE ORTIZ, PARISH PRIEST OF OLAGUE, AGE SEVENTY-ONE [FOL. 37R–V]

He is the first cousin of Juan de Unciti. . . . Since Unciti and Alzate were first married, he has never seen Unciti lay a hand on her, but rather has seen him treat her well by word and deed. . . . Unciti's wife does not govern herself well and is negligent with money. She squanders the household and does not pay attention to its business; this witness knows about it because her husband took away the keys to the house. Alzate has left that house four or five times, and she has been taken back by her husband through the intervention of this witness. The husband also took her back because the episcopal visitor ordered it.

---

40. Juan de Unciti called several defense witnesses who ended up undermining his case.

This witness notified [Unciti] of the order provided by Dr. Don Luís de Venegas [in August], who is currently the visitor general [for the bishop of Pamplona], that Unciti and his wife should live together as husband and wife. Juan de Unciti responded that he was ready and willing to receive her as they previously were, and he had not thrown her out of the house, but rather she had left on her own authority.

This witness also notified María de Alzate of the visitor's order [in August 1611], and she said she would consider it. Afterward, she has not wanted to return to live with her husband, and it is plain that she has undertaken this lawsuit as a result. This witness has had her banned from the divine offices for not complying with the episcopal order that she should return to live with her husband once more within three months.

... This witness knows for certain that based on what he has seen from Unciti and those of Unciti's house, the contrary party [Alzate] took the daughter against her father's will to Pamplona, where Alzate has her, and Alzate does not want to bring her here for reasons this witness cannot relay by order of the Holy Inquisition.[41] This witness said that though he was present at the time the litigating parties married, and then when Alzate returned to Olague from Lantz, he did not see or know that she brought anything with her as a dowry except a meager bed, which she took from her husband's house when she left, and this is the truth.

JUANA DE MAYA, AGE FIFTY-TWO, WIFE OF MIGUEL DE
OYEREGUI, WOODWORKER[42] [FOLS. 38V–39R]
She has lived with her husband in the house that borders Unciti's for more than thirty-two years. From the time the litigants married until the time that Alzate left her husband's house, this witness has

41. Inquisitor Salazar had told the priest Ortiz that no one in Olague should speak about witches under pain of excommunication. In fact, it appears that Olague's villagers continued to discuss witches after Salazar's departure and only mentioned his order of silence when it was to their advantage to do so.

42. Juana de Maya's son with Miguel de Oyeregui, Guillendo, had been forced into false confessions and accusations of witchcraft in May and June 1611; see chapter 2. Given Juan de Unciti's role in those false confessions and accusations—for he was the one who allegedly threatened to club the Oyeregui child to death—it seems odd that the child's mother, Juana de Maya, was presented by Unciti as a potential witness in his favor.

known how often Unciti verbally abused Alzate. This witness saw and perceived from her house how he was accustomed to mistreat her, putting his hands on her face and person, causing scandal and gossip in the village on account of people seeing her with marks of the blows that he gave her. This witness never saw a reason or fault in Alzate that would have provoked the mistreatment and miserable life that her husband gave her, because she behaved in all ways like an honorable and proper wife, serving and working like any other wife in Olague, except that on certain occasions and quarrels, she talked back to her husband.

This witness has seen Alzate taken back in by her husband three or four times, through the mediation of certain persons, after Alzate left his house. The last time that Alzate left [August 1611], she told this witness that she had departed because her husband's household had given her the reputation of a witch when she was not one. And this witness saw that later, her husband wanted to receive her into his house and she did not want to go, saying that she would rather live alone in poverty rather than have such a miserable life as she had formerly endured. . . .

This witness said that she had heard Alzate say various times that she had taken the daughter from her second marriage to Pamplona, where she would stay. At the time that Alzate married her second husband, she brought no more dowry than a single bed, because Unciti was willing to take her alone. This witness knows that Alzate took the bed with her when she left Unciti's house.

ESTEBANIA DE ARANAZ, WIDOW OF BELTRÁN DE LARREA,
AGE EIGHTY [FOLS. 39R–40V]
. . . She has lived with Unciti and Alzate and never saw a thing, just the usual disagreements between husband and wife. She saw Alzate leave her husband's house four or five times, and Alzate was received back through the mediation of this witness, along with other people. . . .

The last time Alzate left [August 1611], her husband said, "What happened in the past is enough. Stay in the house without roaming," and Alzate left anyway with her bed. Alzate is a hotheaded woman, who is accustomed to talk back to her husband and his children [from his first marriage], and sometimes she is disrespectful, particularly toward Don Martín de Unciti who is a deacon. . . . Alzate brought nothing to the marriage but a bed. This witness never saw Unciti call Alzate a witch or any other rude term, but their daughter [Marimartín] said the mother was a witch and had made her into a witch, and this is all this witness knows.

FELIPE DE EGOZCUE, AGE TWENTY-EIGHT [FOLS. 40V–41R]

. . . He said that last year [August 1611], when he was the magistrate [*regidor*] of Olague, María de Alzate came to his house, on a day he cannot recall. She told him that she did not want to live with her husband because of the miserable life he gave her; she wanted to leave his house, and asked this witness to accompany her as the magistrate to her husband's house. This witness accompanied her there. Alzate told her husband that his son had kicked her and she did not want to live with him. . . . And thus she wanted to take her bed. Her husband replied that the past was enough, and she should not walk around with such crazy ideas. Then, in the presence of this witness, Alzate took the bed from the house and carried it with her, and this is the truth and what this witness knows.

JUAN DE ZOZAYA, AGE FORTY-NINE [FOL. 41R–V][43]

. . . After the last episcopal visitor came through the parish church—on a day he does not remember—the parish priest of Olague, Pedro de Ortiz, took this witness with him to Juan de Unciti's house, saying that he had to notify him of an order given by the visitor. The order said that within a certain number of days, Unciti had to live with his wife. The parish priest notified Unciti of the order in the presence of this witness, and Unciti replied that he would obey the mandate and was ready to comply with it. He was ready to live with his wife, wanting to receive her, and nothing would be lacking on his part. He said she had left the house against his will. This is the truth.

43. Zozaya was the constable (*jurado*) of Olague whom Don Pedro de Echaide charged with dereliction of duty in June 1611. See chapter 3.

THE VERDICT, FEBRUARY 20, 1612 [FOL. 53R]

We find that Maria de Alzate has proven well and completely her intention, as a result of which we must declare that they shall live separately. Juan de Unciti is not to worry or disturb Maria de Alzate, and he must pay costs. Alzate is not prevented from hearing divine offices.

BIBLIOGRAPHY

Alberola, Eva Lara. "El panfleto de don Juan de Mongastón sobre las brujas de Zugarramurdi (Auto de fe de Logroño de 1610), editado en 1611: ¿Documento histórico o literatura?" *Revista del Instituto de Lengua y Cultura Españolas* 33 (2017): 259–82.

Azurmendi, Mikel. *Las brujas de Zugarramurdi*. Pamplona: Editorial Almuzara, 2013.

Berraondo Piudo, Mikel. "La violencia interpersonal en la Navarra moderna (siglos XVI–XVII)." PhD diss., Universidad de Navarra, 2012.

Berraondo Piudo, Mikel, and Félix Segura Urra. *Odiar: Violencia y justicia, siglos XIII–XVI*. Pamplona: Editorial EGN, 2012.

Bettlé, Nicole. "Child-Witches." In *The Routledge History of Witchcraft*, edited by Johannes Dillinger, 233–43. London: Routledge, 2020.

Blécourt, Willem de. "Sabbath Stories: Toward a New History of Witches' Assemblies." In *The Oxford Handbook of Witchcraft in Early Modern Europe and Colonial America*, edited by Brian P. Levack, 84–100. Oxford: Oxford University Press, 2013.

Briggs, Robin. *Witches and Neighbors: The Social and Cultural Context of European Witchcraft*. New York: Viking, 1996.

Caro Baroja, Julio. "De nuevo sobre la historia de brujería." *Príncipe de Viana* 30 (1969): 265–328.

Clark, Stuart. *Thinking with Demons: The Idea of Witchcraft in Early Modern Europe*. Oxford, UK: Clarendon Press, 1997.

Fernández Nieto, Manuel. *Proceso a la brujería: En torno al auto de fe de los brujos de Zugarramurdi, Logroño 1610*. Madrid: Tecnos, 1989.

Flynn, Maureen. "Mimesis of the Last Judgment: The Spanish *Auto de Fe*." *Sixteenth Century Journal* 22 (1991): 281–97.

García-Arenal, Mercedes. "A Polyphony of Voices: Trials and Graffiti of the Prisons of the Inquisition in Palermo." *Quaderni Storici* 157 (2018): 39–70.

Geschiere, Peter. "Witchcraft and the Dangers of Intimacy: Africa and Europe." In *Emotions in the History of Witchcraft*, edited by Laura

Kounine and Michael Ostling, 213–29. London: Palgrave Macmillan, 2016.

Goñi Gaztambide, José. *Los navarros en el Concilio de Trento y la reforma tridentina en la diocesis de Pamplona*. Pamplona: Imprenta diocesana, 1947.

Hagen, Rune Blix. "Witchcraft Criminality and Witchcraft Research in the Nordic Countries." In *The Oxford Handbook of Witchcraft in Early Modern Europe and Colonial America*, edited by Brian P. Levack, 375–92. Oxford: Oxford University Press, 2013.

Henningsen, Gustav. *The Salazar Documents*. Leiden: Brill, 2004.

———. *The Witches' Advocate*. Reno: University of Nevada Press, 1980.

Homza, Lu Ann. *The Spanish Inquisition, 1478–1614: An Anthology of Sources*. Indianapolis: Hackett, 2006.

———. *Village Infernos and Witches' Advocates: Witch-Hunting in Navarre, 1608–1614*. University Park: Pennsylvania State University Press, 2022.

———. "When Witches Litigate: New Sources from Early Modern Navarre." *Journal of Modern History* 91 (2019): 245–75.

Idoate, Florencio. *La brujería en Navarra y sus documentos*. Pamplona: Diputación Foral de Navarra, 1978.

Kamen, Henry. *The Spanish Inquisition: A Historical Revision*. New Haven: Yale University Press, 1997.

Kivelson, Valerie A. "'So That They Will Love Me and Pine for Me': Intimacy and Distance in Early Modern Russian Magic." In *Emotions in the History of Witchcraft*, edited by Laura Kounine and Michael Ostling, 117–35. London: Palgrave Macmillan, 2016.

Kors, Alan Charles, and Edward Peters. *Witchcraft in Europe, 400–1700: A Documentary History*. Philadelphia: University of Pennsylvania Press, 2001.

Kounine, Laura, and Michael Ostling, eds. *Emotions in the History of Witchcraft*. London: Palgrave Macmillan, 2016.

Kuehn, Thomas. "Reading Microhistory: The Example of *Giovanni and Lusanna*." *Journal of Modern History* 61 (1989): 512–34.

Lancre, Pierre de. *On the Inconstancy of Witches*. Edited by Gerhild Scholz Williams. Arizona Studies in the Middle Ages and Renaissance 16. Turnhout, Belgium: Brepols, 2006.

Levack, Brian P. *The Witch-Hunt in Early Modern Europe*. London: Longman, 1995.

Maza, Sarah. "Kids Aren't All Right: Historians and the Problem of Childhood." *American Historical Review* 120 (2020): 1261–85.

Monteano Sorbet, Peio J. *El iceberg navarro: Euskera y castellano en la Navarra del siglo XVI*. Pamplona: Pamiela, 2017.

Monter, E. William. *Frontiers of Heresy: The Spanish Inquisition from the Basque Lands to Sicily*. Cambridge: Cambridge University Press, 1990.

Rojas, Rochelle. "Bad Christians and Hanging Toads: Witch Trials in Early Modern Spain, 1525–1675." PhD diss., Duke University, 2016.

———. "The Witches' Apprentice: Toads in Early Modern Navarre." *Sixteenth Century Journal* 51 (2020): 719–40.

Rolley, Thibaut Maus de, and Jan Machielson. "The Mythmaker of the Sabbat: Pierre de Lancre's *Tableau de l'inconstance des mauvais anges et demons.*" In *The Science of Demons: Early Modern Authors Facing Witchcraft and the Devil*, edited by Jan Machielson, 283–98. Abingdon, UK: Routledge, 2020.

Roper, Lyndal. "'Evil Imaginings and Fantasies': Child-Witches and the End of the Witch Craze." *Past and Present* 167 (2000): 107–39.

———. *Witch Craze: Terror and Fantasy in Baroque Germany.* New Haven: Yale University Press, 2006.

Rowlands, Alison "Gender, Ungodly Parents and a Witch Family in Seventeenth-Century Germany." *Past and Present* 232 (2016): 45–86.

———. "Witchcraft and Gender in Early Modern Europe." In *The Oxford Handbook of Witchcraft in Early Modern Europe and Colonial America*, edited by Brian P. Levack, 449–67. Oxford: Oxford University Press, 2013.

Tabernero-Sala, Cristina, and Jesús M. Usunáriz Garayoa, "*Bruja, brujo, hechicera, hechicero, sorguin* como insultos en la Navarra del siglos XVI–XVII." In *Modelos de vida y cultura en Navarra (siglos XVI y XVII): Antología de textos*, edited by Mariela Insúa, 381–429. Pamplona: Servicio de Publicaciones de la Universidad de Navarra, 2016.

Tausiet, María. *Urban Magic in Early Modern Spain: Abracadabra Omnipotens.* Palgrave Historical Studies in Witchcraft and Magic. London: Palgrave Macmillan, 2014.

Taylor, Scott K. *Honor and Violence in Golden-Age Spain.* New Haven: Yale University Press, 2008.

Usunáriz Garayoa, Jesús M. "La caza de brujas en la Navarra moderna (siglos XVI–XVII)." In "Akelarre: La caza de brujas en el Pirineo (siglos XIII–XIX): Homenaje al Professor Gustav Henningsen." Special issue, *Revista Internacional de los Estudios Vascos* 9 (2012): 306–50.

Voltmer, Rita. "The Witch in the Courtroom: Torture and the Representations of Emotion." In *Emotions in the History of Witchcraft*, edited by Laura Kounine and Michael Ostling, 97–116. London: Palgrave Macmillan, 2016.

Willumsen, Liv Helene. "Children Accused of Witchcraft in 17th Century Finnmark." *Scandinavian Journal of History* 38 (2013): 18–41.

INDEX

"act of faith" ceremony. See *auto de fe* ceremony (1610)

akelarres (Devil's gatherings)
   accounts from *auto de fe*, 27, 28, 29–31
   accusation against Miguel de Imbuluzqueta, 43, 44, 63–64, 65, 67
   accusations against Olagüe family, 74, 75–76, 78, 86, 87, 103
   described, 1–2, 22, 24, 24n24
   in Elizondo, 35, 36
   in Zubieta, 37

Alzate, Domingo de, 94, 103, 109

Alzate, Juan de, 45–47, 92

Alzate, María de
   accusations against, 13–14, 101–2, 103–7, 111
   petition for marital separation, 101–2, 108–11, 112–15, 116–21, 122
   trial of Miguel de Imbuluzqueta, 40, 42–43, 45, 46–47, 52–53, 55, 58–59
   See also petition for marital separation

Antoco, Catalina de, 18, 21–22

Anzu, María de, 82

Aranaz, Estebania de, 120–21

Araníbar, Leon de, 18, 31–38

Aritzu, Brigida de, 113

Arizu, Pedro de, 37

Arraioz, village of, ix, 12n29, 18, 33

Arraíz, Miguel de, 54–56

Ascarraga, Juan de, 52–54

auto de fe ceremony (1610)
   account from, 17, 18, 25–31
   described, 5–6
   increase in witchcraft following, 97n42

Azcarraga, Juan de, 80–81, 94

Barrenechea, Graciana de, 18, 19n10, 20, 33–34

Barrenechea, María Chipía de, 27

Basque, legal documentation in, 14–15, 20n11

Becerra Holguín, Juan de, 17, 18–20

bigamy, 4

cannibalism, 2, 30–31, 48n21, 55–56, 58

canon *Episcopi*, 19n8

Catholic Mass, inversion of, 1–2

child witches
   centrality in witch hunts, xi, 9, 11–12
   Navarrese witchcraft traditions and, 1–3
   in slander trials, 13–14, 44n10
   Zugarramurdi witch hunt and, 6–7
   See also Echaide-Olagüe trial; Olagüe-Imbuluzqueta trial; petition for marital separation; prior events